CONFRON

A Strategic Management Simulation

CANADIAN EDITION

RANDY HOFFMAN
DIRK K. BECKER

Atkinson College, York University

1989

IRWIN
Homewood, Illinois 60430

ISBN 0-256-06940-9

Printed in Canada

1 2 3 4 5 6 7 8 9 0 WBC 6 5 4 3 2 1 0 9

Acknowledgements

The CONFRONTATION project began in 1979 with a modest, computer-based strategic exercise. The present simulation, which bears only a passing resemblance to our earliest primitive efforts, owes much of its development to those who have helped us throughout the last 9 years. First, we wish to thank our colleagues in the Administrative Studies Department, Atkinson College, York University for their helpful suggestions concerning how the principles of accounting, finance, marketing, and production could be accurately incorporated in this experiential learning tool. We also appreciate the work done on our behalf by Geoffrey Jones of Seneca College, particularly for proposing student planning aids and alterations to our user interface. Iven Zanardo, a teaching assistant, offered a number of constructive suggestions and proposed the algorithm for the production capacity learning curve. Bo Yin Chu, one of our students, spent many hours patiently checking and rechecking the functioning of the program. Finally, over the years participants freely gave suggestions and critical comments, many of which are now embodied in CONFRONTATION.

For the preparation of this Participant's Manual, we are indebted to June Bradford who transformed illegible scratchings into text, and to Pauline Lai, whose expert typesetting produced the book you are now reading.

The Authors

Preface

The first purpose of strategic business simulation is to enhance the student's understanding of the various management disciplines by providing the opportunity to integrate and apply theoretical knowledge in a dynamic environment. Participating in a simulation such as CONFRONTATION may be as close as it is possible to come to a real world management experience within the confines of a traditional course of study. Unlike passive business cases, where the situation can never react to the student's analysis, CONFRONTATION offers an almost unlimited variety of strategic problems that result directly from the decisions and actions of all participants. Unlike the real world, however, the simulation enables total concentration upon strategic planning, as the implementation of those plans is carried out by a computer—simulating a year's operations within a few seconds. Also unlike the real world, CONFRONTATION is ultimately only a learning experience. No participant's performance will affect his or her standard of living. Creative strategies may be freely tested with a degree of freedom not available when the welfare of a real corporation and its employees depend upon the outcome.

CONFRONTATION is a model of a competition between three firms in the sense that the salient strategic elements are present, but many thousands of tactical or operational details, which must be attended to in reality, are absent. This facilitates a time compression so that students can participate in the entire life cycle of their corporation over a relatively short period. In this way, an appreciation of the impact of strategy upon results, and the way strategic options are constrained by dynamic internal and environmental situations will become apparent to all participants.

Finally, the authors wish to express their hope that students will enjoy their experience with CONFRONTATION. In academic courses or a career, you will perform and learn best when you enjoy what you are doing.

COMPANY NAME ______________________

\# ______________________

	NAME	Telephone
President	______________________	__________
Marketing Manager	______________________	__________
Production Manager	______________________	__________
Engineering Manager	______________________	__________
Design Manager	______________________	__________
Analysts	______________________	__________
	______________________	__________
	______________________	__________
	______________________	__________

Table of Contents

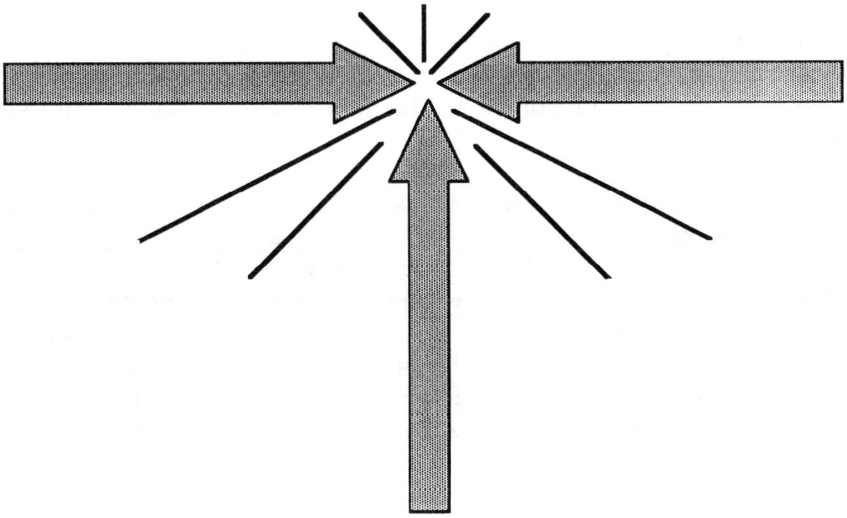

PART I – DESCRIPTION OF CONFRONTATION

1. INTRODUCTION TO CONFRONTATION

This is a simulation of the operation of three firms in a competitive (oligopolistic) environment. Each firm produces only electronic **timer/programmers** to operate lights, appliances, or other electrical devices for the home market. The products are about the size of a large pocket calculator, and they all display the current time digitally. By scrolling start and stop times, one or more household devices may be automatically switched on or off. The more expensive of these timer/programmers offer keypad entry of times, control several outlets independently, and offer an audible alarm feature. Development now completed will enable the highest quality devices to be programmed remotely by calling in to your home telephone. These products are sold directly to consumers via direct mail or newspaper advertising across Canada by firms located in Quebec, Southern Ontario, and Alberta.

At the beginning of the CONFRONTATION simulation, each firm is in a startup situation. Production, Engineering, Research and Marketing departmental staffs have been assembled chiefly from other firms in the electronics industry. Each of the three firms have identical resources with which to begin the simulation. CONFRONTATION consists of a limited series of yearly product introductions by each firm. Price, advertising, investment in corporate resources, and external financing may be controlled within certain limits. Briefly, CONFRONTATION takes place as follows. The management (students) of each firm collaborate to arrive at a set of decisions that is their company's strategy for the next year. These decisions are submitted simultaneously by each firm to the simulation instructor (in writing or by floppy disk) who enters them into the computer that is operating the simulation program. Based upon the relative effectiveness of each firm's strategy to deal with their internal, market, and competitive factors, the program will calculate a complete set of yearly operational results for each company. The bottom line of these results, Net Profit, is the most important determinant of success.

Successful strategies require an analysis of the available market, assessment of the resource strengths of competitors, and estimation of their future strategic decisions based upon previous behaviour and their available options. Generic strategies of cost leadership, focus (market niching) or differentiation must be considered and employed when appropriate. A firm that is consistently (market niche) more successful during a series of product introductions will, through accumulation of profits or through suffering less losses, be able to command greater resources than its competitors. Consequently, the leading firm will be able to dominate the market, and in cases of large differences in resources, cause its competitors to suffer bankruptcy, or possibly acquire them in a financial takeover.

CONFRONTATION will end when (1) the preannounced number of years has been simulated, or (2) before that time, if the dominant firm has taken over, or driven both of its competitors into bankruptcy. It is also possible that all firms produce losses. Then, the dominant or winning firm is the one that loses the least amount of its starting capital; and has the least negative retained earnings.

When a firm has a profitable year, one or more of its management team may receive a profit sharing bonus. When profit sharing occurs and the simulation has ended, the winning individual will be the one who has accumulated the largest bonus.

2. COMPANY STRUCTURE

To form its management group, each firm needs a group of about five to eight students. It is not required to have the same number of students in each firm. The roles each student assumes are mutually decided upon by the group, once it has been formed. However, each company should first get acquainted, if necessary; and then elect a president who can chair the meeting in order to select positions for all other participants.

Management Roles for Each Firm

President
Analysts (0–3 persons)
Marketing Manager
Production Manager
Engineering Manager
Design Manager

Role Descriptions

President

The president will have **primary** responsibility for acquisition of debt, issue of equity, takeover of competitors, allocation of budgetary funds to departments, and co-ordination of their strategic planning activities. This role, therefore, has overall responsibility for formulation, co-ordination and implementation of corporate strategy. As leader of the general management group, the president is also responsible for the achievement of goals and the correction of strategy. The president, however, should not coerce the managers—it is intended that power-sharing and group decision-making will be employed to a significant extent. The president does have **sole authority** to acquire debt capital, issue additional equity, invest surplus funds, takeover competitors, and to make the final decision concerning departmental budgets.

Following are **suggested** roles for the rest of the management group:

Analysts

Provide analytical assistance to the president. Analysts are assigned tasks by the president. Analysts may specialize in providing analytical assistance to specific functional areas, such as marketing and finance, or specific strategic functions, such as constructing economic scenarios and forecasting results. As there is no Manager of Finance, an analyst could be appointed to fulfil that function.

Marketing Manager

Primary responsibility[1] for: selecting a market segment and setting product price, advertising, market surveys, sales forecasts, and requesting a departmental budget. The marketing manager must take the generic strategic direction that is decided upon and translate it into specific marketing policies. As with each department, the marketing manager coordinates policies with the other functional areas.

Production Manager

Primary responsibility for minimum order and planned production decisions, capital equipment expenditures, inventory management and requesting a departmental budget. The production manager must ensure that there is adequate production capacity to serve the likely range of sales volumes. On the other hand, excess capacity that ties up capital and causes excessive expenses to be incurred must be avoided.

Engineering Manager

Primary responsibility for requesting a departmental budget, raw material quality selection, and assisting the production manager in determining minimum order size, planned production run decisions, and capital equipment expenditures to ensure adequate synergy and production capacity. Raw material price is critical to the generic strategy selected. Focus, differentiation, and price leadership all require an appropriate selection.

---

1 Primary responsibility does not mean sole authority which is negotiated among all managers and the president.

Design Manager — Primary responsibility for requesting departmental budgets, market segment selection, and assisting the marketing manager in evaluating and projecting competitors' activities with respect to their product offerings. This manager's main strategic contribution is to recommend approaches to product design (segment, features, price, quality) that enable the exploitation of competitive opportunities.

It will be necessary to monitor the same activities being carried out by competitors to gain insight into their likely future strategies. After each yearly simulation, all decisions made by the three firms will become known along with the performance results. All departmental managers must cooperate in analyzing competitive and market information as a necessary input to the planning process.

Human Resource Management

As CONFRONTATION is a computer-based simulation most of your company's staff is fictional. However, this does not mean that human resource issues will be trivial and that you cannot encounter any serious problems.

The **real** human resources your firm must deal with are the participants who are taking the roles of mangers. Since the president has no opportunity to use coercive measures to control the management group, power must be shared to a large extent, and a people-oriented leadership style should be practiced. Sensitivity to the preferences and competencies of all participants is the best means to obtain full participation.

Certainly, each person will possess skills, abilities, and insights that will be, at least to some extent, unique. As in all real organizations, there will be an optimal way to allocate the tasks and synthesize individual actions into an effective strategic plan. The final output of the process is the set of strategic decisions that determines how your firm performs in the competitive market. There are literally billions of possible strategies that could be employed (when considering the practical range of each strategic variable). Selecting the best strategy cannot be performed automatically by trial and error. It is best accomplished by a rigorous exercise of strategic planning (see Part II) carried out by all participants in a cooperative atmosphere. The generation and maintenance of this atmosphere is the chief human resource challenge of the CONFRONTATION simulation.

Financial Structure

Each company commences operations with an equal amount of startup capital [(a) ________][2] that will be announced by the simulation instructor. This capital shall be used to acquire and maintain company resources, as well as to finance yearly product introductions by providing funds for raw materials and promotional expenses. Initially, that amount of capital comprises a firm's total assets. By the beginning of the first year's simulation, however, it will be necessary to purchase production equipment and to hire employees to staff each department. Profitable operations resulting from successful competitive strategies will increase asset value (and equity).

---

2 See appendix II to Part I, p. 25, where simulation parameters (a) should be recorded as announced by the simulation instructor.

Generally speaking, when one firm's assets significantly exceeds those of its competitors, that firm is likely to become dominant and win the simulation. As in real world situations, a firm with superior financial assets has a broader choice of generic strategic alternatives that may give it a substantial competitive advantage. Examples of alternatives available to relatively wealthy firms include:

1. Substantial investments in appropriate company resources to effect a higher quality product, along with substantial promotional expenditures (product differentiation and/or focus strategy).
2. Offering a higly attractive price, even planning for a loss on operations which will then be experienced by all firms, but which can better afforded by the wealthier firm (price leadership, possibly predatory pricing).
3. Threatening competitors with a takeover causing them to employ defensive strategies that may not be profitable (a diversionary financial strategy).

The wealthier firm has a broader choice of strategic options while poorer companies are restricted, and thus are more predictable. If it becomes possible for a firm to predict the strategy of competitors while it remains less predictable, itself, it is easier for it to continue performing well and increase the difference in corporate wealth. Over a series of yearly product introductions, this trend may tend to accelerate.

Debt

During any product introduction, a firm may borrow from an already established line of credit as long as that loan does not bring the firm's debt-equity ratio[3] above 40%. Afterwards, if a firm suffers losses (reducing retained earnings and, therefore, equity) which brings its debt-equity ratio above 70%, compulsory repayment to reduce it to 70% **must** occur—even if the result is bankruptcy. This is because creditors will become alarmed at the degree of leverage and would prefer to liquidate the company at that moment rather than wait to see if performance can be improved. For the simulation, all loans and loan payments are made when the next set of strategic decisions are submitted. Under the circumstances of an unacceptable debt-equity ratio, compulsory loan repayment would be required before a firm can sell the next year's product offering to raise additional funds. Firms do not have to retain sufficient cash to pay for raw materials for a full year's production, as it is assumed that suppliers will offer credit until sales revenues are received. However, when production goes into inventory and is not sold that year, all suppliers must be paid in full by the year end.

The Simulation Instructor will announce the interest rate charged on borrowed funds [(b) ______________ See p. 25].

Equity

Each firm has already issued and sold one million common shares to raise its starting capital. Starting at the beginning of year 3, it may then issue part of an additional one million shares each year—not more than [(c) ______________ See p. 25] at one time—in order to raise further capital. The market value of these share offerings is given by the following:

$$\text{Market Price per Share} = 8[2.2\overline{\text{EPS}} - \text{VAR}][\text{prev. total \# of shares/new total \# of shares}]$$

---

3 Defined as: debt/(debt + equity)

where $\overline{EPS}$ is the average net earnings per share for the firm (after tax); and VAR is the variance of those earnings per share. For example, suppose a firm at the third product introduction wishes to raise capital through offering an additional 400,000 shares. In the first two years, assume its net results were a \$100,000 loss and \$380,000 profit, respectively. The average net earnings, $\overline{E}$, are therefore:

$$\overline{E} = \frac{-\$100{,}000 + \$380{,}000}{2} = \$\ 140{,}000$$

or, since 1 million shares were issued originally, $\overline{EPS}$ would be \$0.14 per share.

The standard statistical formula for variance would give:

$$VAR = \sum_{i=1}^{n} \frac{(EPS_i - \overline{EPS})^2}{n} = \frac{(-.10 - .14)^2}{2} + \frac{(.38 - .14)^2}{2}$$

$$= .0576$$

$$\text{Market Price per Share} = 8[(2.2 \times \$\ .14) - .0576][1{,}000{,}000/1{,}400{,}000]$$

$$= \$\ 1.431$$

By selling 400,000 shares, therefore, the firm would receive \$572,343 in additional capital. Since the usual range of starting capital is between 3 and 7 million dollars, note that a market price of about \$1.43 per share is less than the starting book value. The latter term in the market price per share equation has the effect of maintaining the same price-earnings ratio for all shares issued after the new issue has been sold. As the amount of additional shares a firm decides to issue is increased, the price the market is willing to pay decreases. This is because each additional share represents a dilution of the ownership of the company. The return a shareholder might expect to receive would be diminished by an expansion in the number of shares outstanding.

In the formula for calculating the market value of additonal share offerings, the VAR term accounts for the risk inherent in the firm's performance. Potential investors would be worried about the large fluctuations in previous yearly earnings, because it suggests that future earnings might also be uncertain. When the variance of earnings is sufficiently large, the share value may be calculated as negative (effectively zero value) even though the average earnings per share is positive. It would be advantageous to offer shares at the point where the prior average earnings per share is high and the variance in earnings is low. Obviously, if the average EPS is negative, no share offerings can be made (although debt may possibly be employed to raise funds).

Reasons for raising additional funds include financing the purchase of capital equipment, enabling heavier investments in product introductions, facilitating the acquisition of a competitor, blocking your acquisition by a competitor, or protecting your firm from future bankruptcy. The advantage of employing share offerings to raise capital is that there are no dividend payments necessary on common stock; whereas interest must be paid on debt owing, and poor performance may result in your firm being forced to repay and/or liquidate its assets in bankruptcy. The decision of when to issue shares must also reflect the strategic consideration mentioned above, that greater financial resources enable more freedom in the choice of strategies—a competitive advantage. Finally, since the winning firm shall be the one with the highest equity among the competitors, a successful share issue prior to the final year's product introduction may assist in the achievement of that goal.

3. DEPARTMENT BUDGETS – RESOURCE EFFECTIVENESS

Budgetary Allocations

A firm must allocate at least a minimum amount [(d) __________ See p. 25], to each departmental budget, yearly, to support its operation. This is a basic level that at least would enable the company to operate the department with minimal resources. Principally, the amount covers salaries. It is unlikely that your firm will compete effectively unless more substantial investments are employed in most cases.

The ratio between any two departmental allocations (capital equipment is not included) must not exceed 2.5:1 within any firm. This provision simply reflects that all functional areas require balanced amounts of resources within the firm. Regardless of the amount allocated to each department (and not governed by the 2.5:1 ratio), $250,000 will automatically be allocated for general and administrative overhead. The total that may be allocated for departmental budgets, advertising, market surveys, and capital equipment is limited to the firm's liquid assets. However, these may be increased by borrowing or issuing more shares when these measures are possible.

Departmental budgetary allocations support and renew the resource base of your firm, and thereby help create the synergy by which profit may be generated. They include marketing overhead, production overhead, engineering overhead, and design overhead. Half of the production allocation is a direct cost charged to manufacturing. Capital equipment purchases also contribute to the synergy of the Production Department and production capacity. Advertising can be employed to improve marketing effectiveness, and a selection of more expensive raw materials will enhance the engineering resource effectiveness. The effect of those factors will be explained below.

Resource Effectiveness

Resources, by their presence alone, do not create performance. It depends upon synergy. That is, the effectiveness with which the system's resources interact—both internally among themselves, and externally with environmental factors such as the market, raw material suppliers, etc. . . . Synergy in real corporations, depends upon the selection and deployment of resources, and especially the competence with which they are managed. In CONFRONTATION, synergy is simulated by the application of modifiers called Resource Effectiveness (RE) factors to departmental investments. Companies in the simulation cannot directly influence the RE factors. However, by making appropriate strategic choices after the first year it is possible to make the best of whatever synergy is likely to be obtained.

At the beginning of the simulation (the first year's product introduction), each firm is in a startup condition and the synergy available within each department is unknown. The Resource Effectiveness Factors (RE Factors) are then chosen at random according to the probability distributions given below. In subsequent years, the factors can alter slowly from their starting values as they do in real organizations that experience changes in resource effectiveness throughout their existence. Thus, a department manager may find that the synergy with which his or her department utilizes its resources remains about the same, improves slowly, or degrades slowly from year to year.

This process occurs independently within all departments for all three competitive firms. Since market share obtained may partially depend upon how well each firm can exploit its synergy, each firm may perceive competitive advantages or disadvantages as the simulation proceeds.

These determinations of relative synergy determine how well engineering and design departments conceive and design programmer/timers; how well production manufactures them; and how well marketing can promote the product.

Resource Effectiveness (RE) is calculated as follows:

1. The overhead allocations are multiplied by a synergy factor randomly selected (during the first product introduction) according to the following table.

	High Synergy	Medium Synergy	Low Synergy
Marketing	1.70, 30%	1.40, 40%	0.70, 30%
Production	1.55, 20%	1.11, 80%	N/A
Engineering	2.00, 40%	1.70, 50%	1.10, 10%
Design	2.95, 20%	2.40, 50%	0.55, 30%

Note: the first number is the factor, the second is its probability of occurrence.

For example, if \$250,000 was allocated to the marketing department, and the medium synergy random factor of 1.40 occurred, then the Marketing Department Resource Effectiveness would be:

$$RE = 1.40 \times \$250{,}000 = 350{,}000$$

(It is 40% likely that any firm's marketing department experiences this factor during the first year's product introduction.)

However, for the remaining three departments, additional influences are involved.

2. For Production, Resource Effectiveness is given by:

$$(\text{Allocation} \times (\text{Net Value of Capital Equipment})^{.6})^{.6} \times (\text{synergy factor})$$

For example, if \$250,000 was allocated to the Production Department, if the net capital equipment investment was \$500,000, and if the medium synergy factor of 1.11 occurred, then the Production Resource Effectiveness would be:

$$RE = (\$250{,}000 \times (\$500{,}000)^{.6})^{.6} \times 1.11 = 216{,}600$$

The budgetary allocation mainly supports the salary of Production Deparment employees. Both workers and capital equipment are required for the production department and they jointly influence production RE (synergy).

Purchasing additional capital equipment will therefore increase the resource effectiveness of the Production Department, although with sharply diminishing marginal returns.

3. For Engineering and Design, Resource Effectiveness is given by:

$$\text{Allocation} \times \frac{(\text{raw material cost})^{.75}}{(\text{product price})^{.75}} \times (\text{synergy factor})$$

For example, if $250,000 was allocated to the Design Department, if the ratio of raw material cost to product price was .5, and if the 2.40 synergy factor occurred, then the Design Resource Effectiveness would be:

$$RE = \$250{,}000 \times (.5)^{.75} \times 2.40 = 356{,}762$$

The quality of the raw material components greatly affects the product's appearance (design), functioning, and reliability. For any given overhead allocation to support fixed resources in the Engineering and Design departments, it is easier to produce a product that will be perceived by the market to be of high quality relative to its price, if the raw materials selected are themselves of high quality. Of course, as the cost of raw materials approaches the selling price, the contribution margin becomes smaller and corporate sales, even though large, will become unprofitable, at least in the short run.

When the raw material cost selected equals or exceeds $56.00, remote (by telephone) entry of commands to the electronic timer/programmer becomes possible due to the purchase of the necessary components. In that case the firm can achieve a product focus on that feature, and its engineering and design resource effectiveness is twice what it would otherwise be. As will be seen below, this may benefit a firm that must compete with another in the high quality market segment, or wishes to differentiate its market image from low quality segment products.

Changes in Synergy

During the second and subsequent product introductions, a new random synergy factor for each department is selected according to the probability distributions above. The synergy factor that will then apply is a weighted average calculated as follows:

$$\text{New Factor} = (.5 \times \text{New Random Synergy Factor}) + (.5 \times \text{Previous Synergy Factor})$$

Because the Previous Synergy Factor will differ for each department within each company, managers will perceive competitive advantages or disadvantages regarding their available synergy of resource use in their department during the next yearly product introduction. Total Resource Effectiveness for the entire firm may be maximized by investing heaviest where such advantages exist. The degree of synergy obtained in each department should influence the adoption of price and market segment strategies. For example, if production synergy is likely to be high, the purchase of additional capital equipment may be very cost effective.

A firm with adequate financial resources may be able to overcome poor synergy by heavy investment. However, this may lead to reduced profits or losses.

Total Resource Effectiveness

By adding the Resource Effectiveness for each department within a given company, Total Resource Effective (TRE) is obtained. TRE is a measure of how well each company's resources have performed in total. Since the market's perception of the product reflects the degree of synergy obtained within each firm, TRE directly affects market penetration when two or more firms are competing in a **single market segment**. The product quality as perceived by the market influences brand preferences.

4. MARKETING AND SALES

Market Demand and Advertising

Figure 1 shows a two segment market demand curve. The shallow negative slope of the curve reflects the non-essential nature of timer/programmers as a household accessory. This is called high price elasticity. It means that as the selling price is increased, demand falls off quite rapidly. Also, as is often the case with this sort of product, those interested in a higher priced (and presumably higher quality) model are less sensitive to price than those who would purchase a lower cost unit with lesser attributes. Therefore, the demand curve for the high quality market segment has a steeper slope. The purchasers of these units typically have a larger disposable income and are less concerned with the price of their purchases. The equation for the segment with low elasticity of demand is $Q = 150{,}000 - 1000P$ (for $P > \$60$); for the high elasticity segment $Q = 510{,}000 - 7000P$ (for $P \leq \$60$): where Q is total market demand in units, and P is price. Each firm must decide yearly which market segment to enter. The minimum price is $10.

Potential purchasers of a higher priced model will buy the lower priced offering instead, if the former is not available. Purchasers who prefer a lower price, however, will not be attracted to the high price segment. When there are offerings in both segments, sales in the higher segment are determined by that segment's demand curve and are subtracted from the lower segment's sales quantity. The amount subtracted is that purchased by those buyers who are already satisfied with higher quality offerings.

Advertising will stimulate additional demand that will further affect market size (See Market Penetration below). The **Effective** amount of Advertising is 65% of the current year's advertising plus 35% of the previous year's Effective Advertising (or 17.5% of the previous year's Effective Advertising if the firm has entered its product in a different market segment from the previous year). This reflects the fact that advertising does not create brand awareness nor does it influence purchase decisions immediately. Also, its influence does not disappear the moment that new advertising ceases to appear. In the first year, the latency term is zero, and the effective advertising for any firm is 65% of their first year's expenditure. Advertising in one market segment will only stimulate demand in that segment and may, as explained below, limit sales in the other segment.

Alternate Market Sizes

It is never possible to know the exact size of a market. Changing consumer preferences, availability of substitutes, general economic conditions, and other factors will affect the total market that is available to all competitors. This is simulated by the possibility of a high market occurring. (See Figure 1, where it is shown as the upper set of lines in each market segment.)

For the High Market, the equations are:

$$Q = 220{,}000 - 1000P \text{ for } P > \$60 \text{ (higher quality segment)}$$
$$Q = 580{,}000 - 7000P \text{ for } P \leq \$60 \text{ (lower quality segment)}$$

In any year, the probability that the alternate market will occur is 38%. If it does occur, then sales and profits, especially in the higher quality segment, will be significantly increased.

Market Survey

To forecast what size market may occur with greater accuracy (although excluding the effects of advertising), each firm may optionally hire consultants to conduct a market survey. The fee for this work is $200,000 and the results are 90% accurate. For example, if the high market **is** going to occur, it is 90% likely that the survey will predict that event. It does **not** mean that if the survey predicts the High Market, it is 90% likely that it will occur. Forecasts will achieve less than their rated accuracy when predicting unlikely events and vice versa. (See Bayes Theorem in probability theory for a mathematical formulation.) The less likely event is the occurrence of the alternate market (38% probable). The forecast will therefore be less than 90% accurate when predicting this market. Each company hires a different market consultant to estimate the market size (high or normal). Given that it is possible (but not likely) for the survey to be incorrect, two firms could even receive conflicting information.

If a firm decides to purchase a market survey, it will be necessary to formulate two sets of strategic decisions and submit the appropriate one depending upon the survey's prediction. If a firm follows exactly the same strategy no matter what the market survey predicted, it would be of no value. From Figure 1, it can be easily seen that the incidence of a high market has a more dramatic effect upon the high quality segment demand.

Minimum Yearly Sales

During the initial stages of each product introduction, each firm independently carries out a test marketing of a small trial production run in Winnipeg, Manitoba. Each firm advertises in local newspapers and, from the response, estimates what total national sales are likely to be. If this test indicates that sales will be below a minimally acceptable level that a firm specifies for itself, that firm will withdraw its product from the market prior to beginning full scale production and promotional activities. Losses, in that event, will be 60% of the firm's discretionary budgetary allocations and exclude all variable costs and advertising. However, they will include the total cost of the market survey. A capital equipment purchase decision during that year will still be fully implemented, as will interest payments on debt and general and administrative expenses. If there is product inventory from a previous year, it will be discarded. The year is then occupied by product development work with a smaller staff. Many personnel will be laid off. It is necessary for each firm to specify its Minimum Order Size when submitting its yearly strategy. Breakeven analysis may assist in the determination of this quantity. In that case, it would be established at the level where, if sales were lower, greater losses would be incurred by not withdrawing its product. In certain severely competitive situations, or when a firm has made serious strategic errors, this withdrawal option may save millions of dollars.

Note that the test marketing is not part of the market survey that takes place prior to the trial production.

5. MARKET PENETRATION AND SALES

There are 3 factors that **directly** affect market penetration and sales.

1. The Market Segment and price chosen.
2. The Total Resource Effectiveness as reflected in the firm's product.
3. The amount of advertising.

The market penetration achieved by a firm will depend upon these factors, in comparision with the strategy of its competitors. Also, recall that many other factors affect the Total Resource Effectiveness (TRE). Thus, in CONFRONTATION as in the real world, the achievement and maintenance of market penetration is a difficult task requiring careful analysis and planning. To better understand the issue, examine market penetration under each of 4 Cases concerning factor 1. A detailed mathematical treatment is shown in Appendix 1, which can be studied after reading this section.

There are three firms who are simultaneously starting up operations to compete within one another. Each firm can enter either the high quality or the low quality market segment. The following cases represent the particular competitive situation that can arise in the simulation. After one firm has been taken over or has been withdrawn due to bankruptcy, the cases will still apply. However, in the situation where the case refers to two firms sharing of a segment, there may then be only one firm enjoying all the sales. Note also that product quality and attractiveness as represented by the Total Resource Effectiveness will affect the market penetration of one firm when two or more firms are competing for sales within a market segment.

Table 1
The Possible Market Situations that can occur

Case	# of firms intending to enter High Q. Mkt. Seg.	# of firms intending to enter Low Q. Mkt. Seg.	If a firm in the High Q. seg. has lowest Eng. and Des. RE, case becomes:
1	1 firm	2 firms	case 4
2	2 firms	1 firms	case 1
3	3 firms	0 firms	case 2*
4	3 firms or 0 firms	0 firms or 3 firms	not applicable**

* One firm is always demoted to the low quality segment in case 3, which results in a case 2 situation as far as sales calculations are concerned. However, the demoted firm may not be an effective competitor due to its price.

** In case 4, all firms are ending up in the same market segment by intention, or as perceived by the market through demotion.

Case 1

One firm has entered the higher quality (and price) segment and both its engineering and its design Resource Effectiveness (RE) are not the worst among the three competitors. Its sales will be inversely proportional to its price, increased by its own effective advertising, but decreased by the effective advertising of competitors in the other segment. These two competitors will then share a market size which has been decreased by sales in the higher quality segment (which satisfies the demand for a high quality product). Their penetration, relative to each other, will also be affected directly by their TRE values, their prices (inversely), and their amount of Effective Advertising (directly, but with diminishing marginal returns).

Case 2

Two firms are sharing the higher quality segment. Neither has the worst RE in both engineering and design among all three firms. Each of the former two firms' sales will depend upon its TRE, price, and advertising levels as above. Heavy expenditures in advertising by the lower quality segment firm will reduce the higher quality segment's sales in favour of the lower quality segment. In the latter segment, sales of the firm entering its product there will not depend on its TRE since it has no competitors within its segment.

Case 3

Three firms intend to introduce their products into the higher quality segment, but one of the three has the lowest RE in both engineering and design. That firm's product is then treated as if it were appealing only to the lower quality segment (with an unrealistically high price). Case 3 then becomes similar to Case 2, except that the firm which was demoted by the perceptions of the market to the lower quality segment may not be able to enjoy sufficient sales to be profitable due to its attempt to charge too high a price for that submarket. To appreciate this latter consideration, extend the lower quality segment's demand curve to the left and note the sharply reduced sales prospects.

Case 4

In all other situations, all three firms are competing within the same market segment, whether they originally intended to do so or not. Each company's sales will be directly proportional to its TRE, inversely to its price, and directly affected by its effective advertising (with diminishing marginal returns).

Interpretation

The price perceived by the market, which is faced by a range of similar products at different prices, will tend toward the lower of the available prices. (The simulation of that perception is accomplished by the calculation of the harmonic mean of two or three prices offered in Appendix 1.) In order to achieve success with the higher quality market segment, it is necessary that both engineering and design resources **not** be the worst among the competitors. Consumers in that segment are sensitive to the perceived product quality difference between a higher and a lower priced offering, which is largely determined by engineering and design effectiveness. Production resource effectiveness mainly affects product reliability (quality control), but it is also closely related to production capacity. Market penetration, in a contested market segment, is directly proportional to Total Resource Effectiveness and, because both market segments are price sensitive, it is inversely proportional to the price charged. This is not the case, however, for a firm that is alone in either of the two market segments. Then, the market does not compare the products and image of that firm with the other two.

If no firm is in the higher quality segment, then its demand will be shifted to the lower quality segment. Otherwise, when one or two firms are in the higher quality segment, that segment's sales are subtracted from the sales in the lower quality segment (which maintains the market size given by the demand curve). To graphically determine the market size with one firm in the market, find the quantity axis coordinate that corresponds to the unit price. With one firm in the higher quality segment and one in the lower, follow the same procedure for the former firm. The market size available to the latter, however, requires that the former's sales quantity be subtracted from a graphically determined quantity of the firm in the lower quality segment. With two of three firms in either market segment, a graphical analysis is still possible. The applicable price is the harmonic mean of the prices of all products in that segment.

Advertising first acts to increase or decrease the demand (market size) in the market as it affects consumer awareness of the products. If segment advertising effectiveness is less than $100,000, the average demand given by the demand curve will **not** be achieved since consumer awareness will be unusually low. The expressions that follow express this effect on demand.

$$\frac{(A_A)^{.15}}{(100{,}000)^{.15}} \quad \text{or} \quad \frac{(A_A + A_B + A_C)^{.15}}{(100{,}000)^{.15}}$$

However, the exponent of .15 indicates that there is a decreasing marginal effectiveness to advertising. That is, as the amount spent by all firms in the high or low market segments increases, a less than proportional increase in market size is experienced. Market **penetration** for firms sharing a market is proportional to advertising raised to the power of .3, or .33 if the focus strategy of remote entry of commands is selected in the upper end of the higher quality segment. (See Appendix 1.) The exponent is much less than 1 due to the fact that some of the consumers who see one firm's advertising will actually end up buying the products of another firm. Therefore, to some extent, a firm will also benefit its competitors if it advertises significantly more than they do. For example, if a firm that shares the higher quality segment with one competitor has $200,000 in effective advertising, while the competitor has $100,000, the market segment size will increase by $(3)^{.15}$, or 18% more than what it would have been with nominal segment advertising that totals $100,000. The former firm's penetration will be increased by $(2)^{.3}$ or 23% more than what it would have been, if it had advertised at the same level as its competitor. Suppose that with equal effective advertising of $100,000, the first firm would have attained a 50% market penetration (due to TRE and price chosen). By spending twice the amount of its competitor, the penetration will increase to only 61.6%. This may be a profitable amount, but extreme levels of advertising would therefore be unprofitable. However, they may be used as a competitive tactic.

Note that the effective amount of advertising for the firm(s) in the high quality market segment is reduced by 30% of the advertising in the lower quality segment. This is because advertising for lower cost products will divert some of the demand that would otherwise be interested in the higher quality offerings. In an extreme situation (within Case 1 or Case 2), heavy advertising in the lower segment could actually cancel the demand in the upper segment, unless there is also sufficient advertising in the latter. This diversion of demand to the lower segment occurs because the advertising for lower priced goods will serve to convince some consumers, who would normally purchase higher priced programmer/timers, that the lower quality offerings would serve their needs adequately.

In terms of Figure 1, effective advertising shifts the demand curve to the right if it is greater than $100,000 per segment, and to the left if it is not. In the low quality segment, dramatic increases in unit sales can be achieved by lowering prices due to the high price elasticity. However, firms in this segment may still wish to advertise significantly in order to attract some of the buyers who might otherwise purchase higher priced products. In the higher quality segment, the much lower elasticity means that advertising is relatively more effective in stimulating additional demand. This may be more important where a focus strategy requires a high price from the buyer.

When a firm, due to its relatively poor resource effectiveness in its Engineering and Design Departments is demoted to low quality segment in the perception of potential buyers, it can be plotted on the dotted extension of the low quality market demand curve of Figure 1 (See below.). Not only will that fact alone diminish potential sales, but it must then compete, with a high priced product, with any competitor in the low quality market segment. Obviously, that is a market situation that will likely lead to very poor performance.

Modes of Market Competition

Intersegment

1. Firms in the low quality segment attempting to pursue a price leadership strategy can advertise heavily to divert demand to their segment from the high quality segment.
2. Firms in the high quality segment following product differentiation or focus (market niche) strategies can also retaliate by attracting buyers to their own segment by heavy promotion. Intersegment competition by advertising is limited by its diminishing effectiveness, where extreme levels will lead to severe losses.
3. Firms in the low quality segment can invest heavily in research and engineering so that the products of a firm in the high quality segment are perceived as functionally inadqequate.

Intrasegment

1. Advertising heavily will create an image of product differentiation that directly affects market penetration between firms in the same segment. This will also benefit the competitive firm to some extent (as mentioned above), unless only the firm advertising heavily has sufficient production capacity to meet the increased demand.
2. Producing a programmer/timer that is perceived to be better or different than the competition as measured by superior TRE. A focus strategy in the high quality segment is an example. It involves the inclusion of a special feature, remote access command ability, to form and exploit a specific market segment.
3. Producing at a lower price (price leadership strategy within a segment) to both stimulate demand and relative market penetration.

Two Firms Competing

When, through bankruptcy or takeover, two firms remain in the market place, the methods of determining market share and advertising effectiveness remain the same. However, it is not then possible for more than two firms to compete in either market segment. If at least one of the two firms tries to enter its product into the higher quality segment, and that firm has the lowest engineering and design resource effectiveness, it will still be demoted just as when there are three competing firms. (See Appendix 1.)

Production Capacity

Production of programmer/timers requires both employees and equipment. An efficient mixture of workers and machinery occurs when there is an approximately equal investment in capital equipment and the workers' yearly salaries (which is most of the budgetary allocation to the production department). This efficiency is reflected in the number of units that can be produced by the department—that is, production capacity. As the facility produces more and more units over the years, efficiency and production capacity also increase due to the growing experience of the firm in this type of assembly. The three factors of people, equipment, and experience are reflected in the following expression:

$$.35 \times (\text{production overhead allocation} \times \text{net value of capital equipment})^{.5} \times \left[\frac{100{,}000 + (\Sigma Q_i)}{100{,}000}\right]^{.2}$$

where ΣQi represents the total production in units for all previous years of operation.

Note that it is never possible to produce more units than current production capacity.

6. RAW MATERIALS AND PRODUCTION QUANTITY

In this simulation, the only variable cost is raw material cost. (Variable costs are those that increase directly in proportion to production. Production, equipment, and personnel and other expenses are considered fixed for the duration of each year.) It is necessary for each firm to forecast its sales at the time it makes a product introduction. If the test market indicates that the sales will exceed the Minimum Order Size, sufficient raw material supplies will be ordered to meet the forecast sales. If the sales that actually occur are the same as the forecast, then the variable cost of supplies will be the raw material cost as a percentage of the selling price, for all units sold. If the sales are less than the forecast, the production will be the same as if the forecasted sales were received, as all supplies have been ordered. Excess production is then inventoried for possible sale in the following year. If the sales are more than the estimate, then the variable cost on the sales overrun will be [(e) _____ % See p. 25] more than planned due to the necessity of obtaining additional raw material supplies on a rush basis.

It is permissible to select a raw material cost as low as [(f) ____ % See p. 25] of the selected selling price. (As stated above, engineering and design resource effectiveness will be affected substantially by this decision.) The reason for this minimum restriction on the raw material cost is that the assembly of a premium product does tend to require more expensive components than does a cheaper, poorer quality unit. If raw material (components) were less than the stated percentage of the selling price, then the market would reject the product as unacceptable for the price demanded. Of course, it is never possible to produce a volume of products greater than the production capacity of your firm.

7. INVENTORY

Unsold products from the year's production will appear on the balance sheet for the year in which they are produced, valued at the amount of their raw material cost plus a pro rata share of one-half the production overhead allocation[4]. In the next year there will be a charge against income of

4 For example, if 1/2 the production was left unsold in inventory at year end, 1/4 of the production allocation would be capitalized in the inventory balance sheet entry.

20% for storage and refurbishing based on the opening inventory balance, if it is to be sold. Sales in the following year shall first be made from this inventory, assuming that the unit price charged for all your products is not more than [(g) ______ % See p. 25] of the inventory's value. If that price is too high or if old inventory exceeds new sales, then excess inventory is discarded, and a storage and disposal cost of 12% is charged against income instead, for that portion of the inventory that is discarded.

The reason that old inventory cannot be sold at a higher markup over cost is that the technology of the field is advancing and year-old goods are unable to compete on an equal footing with the latest designs. Note that if your firm has a relatively large amount of inventory, your next year's strategy might be constrained by the attempt to dispose of it at a profit. However, by habitually ordering fewer raw materials than is likely to be needed—that is, by specifying a small planned production, you may be in a position where your profit margin is being heavily eroded by habitually having to obtain raw materials at the last minute to meet market demand and paying a premium price for them.

Storage costs show that warehouse space must be rented to keep excess production. Refurbishing is mainly a reinspection and testing of inventory prior to sales. Disposal costs are incurred when the inventory is not saleable. Costs involved are for storage and disassembly prior to disposal.

8. NET OPERATING PROFIT OR LOSS

Net Profit = Gross Sales Revenue less:

1. Inventory Costs
2. Raw Materials Costs
3. Departmental Budgetary Allocations
4. General and Administrative Expenses
5. Interest Expense
6. Depreciation Expense
7. Market Survey and Advertising Costs
8. Profit Sharing

NET INCOME = NET OPERATING PROFIT + INVESTMENT INCOME

9. INCOME TAX

In Canada, income tax is normally applied to all corporations. The CONFRONTATION simulation uses a relatively simple formula to calculate tax liability. The firm that is earning modest profits pays no tax. However, if a firm's net income exceeds $1,000,000, then tax must be paid according to the following formula.

$ Income Tax = [(h) _____ % See p. 25] x [Net Income – 1,000,000]

10. FINANCIAL INVESTMENT OPPORTUNITIES

A firm may invest any part of its uncommitted cash in one of two investment opportunities as follows:

A. The return on investment is distributed normally with a mean of [(i) _____ % See p. 25] and a standard deviation of [(j) _____ %].

B. The return on investment is distributed normally with a mean of [(k) _____ %] and a standard deviation of [(l) _____ %].

Committed cash includes all planned expenditures, general and administrative overhead, and one-half of the raw material committment. The latter is in case there is a sizeable inventory at year end, in which case raw material suppliers can not be paid totally from the proceeds of product sales. It is likely that not all of a firm's working capital is required for operations. Rather than allow sizeable amounts of cash resources to be put to no use, each firm should attempt to invest surplus funds. The investment period is for one year and gains (or losses) increase (or decrease) the subsequent year's working capital. Each firm invests in a different investment opportunity.

Note, by reference to Appendix 2, that Investment A offers a relatively modest expected return, but practically no risk of a loss. Alternative B offers the possibility of higher returns on the average, but also a definite possibility of losing a portion of the funds invested.

When a firm has accumulated an amount of working capital well in excess of immediate cash needs, it may be possible to earn as much interest income as net profit from operations.

11. BANKRUPTCY

If a firm's cash assets are insufficient to finance a minimum investment (the minimum departmental allocation, general and administrative expenses, and $10,000 of advertising) in a year's operations, the firm is bankrupt and is withdrawn from operation. However, a firm does not require funds in advance to purchase raw materials, as suppliers will provide it in anticipation of receiving payment from sales revenue.

If bankruptcy is feared, but not yet imminent, a firm may still be able to borrow funds to supplement available cash. It is unlikely that a firm facing this situation would be able to raise significant amounts by an equity issue. A firm will not be able to borrow funds once bankruptcy has been detected. Since this occurs at the end of each year's operations, and borrowing only takes place at the beginning of the year, loans to stave off bankruptcy must be undertaken well in advance.

12. TAKEOVERS

The forced acquisition of a competitor is possible when the acquirer's asset value is [(m) ____ % See p. 25] of a potential acquiree. The cost of an acquisition is 60% of the acquired firm's total assets. In a case when two firms are eligible to acquire a third, the firm with the largest asset

asset value is given the opportunity to acquire first. Acquisitions take place at the end of a year's operations when the performance of all firms has been disclosed.

The acquired firm's debt is added to that of the acquirer. The additional debt may require a repayment in situations when the acquirer's debt/equity ratio then exceeds the 70% limit. The acquired firm's equity is retired and does not appear under shareholders' investment on the acquirer's balance sheet. At the time of acquisition, the acquired firm's inventory is written off the balance sheet as incompatible with the acquiring firm's production. The acquiring firm will receive between 30 and 60 cents (randomly determined) on the dollar for the inventory that is sold below cost in a quick liquidation sale.

The acquired firm is therefore dissolved and takes no further part in the simulation. Planning to acquire other firms and planning to avoid being acquired by a competitor is a necessary part of the strategic decision-making process. A firm that fears acquisition may issue more shares and take on more debit to try to avoid a takeover, while the firm that wishes to make the acquisition can do the same to increase liquid assets for a takeover. A takeover is only possible when the cash in **both** firms is sufficient to buy out the shareholders of the firm to be taken over. Therefore, a takeover is facilitated by raiding the cash available in the acquiree's account. Acquisitions are advantageous when the acquired firm's cash and capital equipment are attractive, as compared to its debt. A favourable acquisition will enable a firm to become more powerful relative to the remaining competitor. However, a bad takeover can drain the acquiring company of cash, depress earnings per share, and limit future performance. Under some circumstances, a firm may acquire both competitors, thereby winning the simulation immediately!

The simulation program will announce to participants that a takeover is possible and ask whether the potential acquiring company is willing to proceed. There will then be an opportunity to look over the latest financial statements of the firm to determine whether it will be beneficial to purchase. Once the decision has been make, it is immediately implemented. The program then displays a revised balance sheet and performance measures of the acquiring firm.

13. PROFIT SHARING

After each product introduction, a portion of the firm's net profits (if any) are placed in individual accounts as follows: (See p. 25 for percentages distributed.)

1. To the president [______ %].
2. To the departmental manager (within the firm) with the largest RE [_____ %].
3. To the analysis group (as a group) when their firm's profit is the largest for all three firms [______ %].
4. Losses are not distributed.

Profit sharing accumulated throughout the simulation will be the basis for deciding the winning individual (or group of individuals if the Analysis Group as a unit holds the largest amount). Presidents may occasionally find that the strategies suggested by Departmental Managers will benefit their own areas (and therefore their personal accounts), but they may not be in the best of interest of the firm as a whole.

14. END OF THE SIMULATION

After a preannounced number of product introductions, the simulation ends. The winning Firm is simply the one with the largest shareholders' equity (common shares plus retained earnings). The winning Individual, if any, is the one with the largest accumulation of profit sharing funds, and is not necessarily from the winning firm. If the Analysis Group wins, each member of that Group will be considered a winning Individual.

The simulation will also be terminated should, through bankruptcy and/or acquisition, only one firm remains to serve the market.

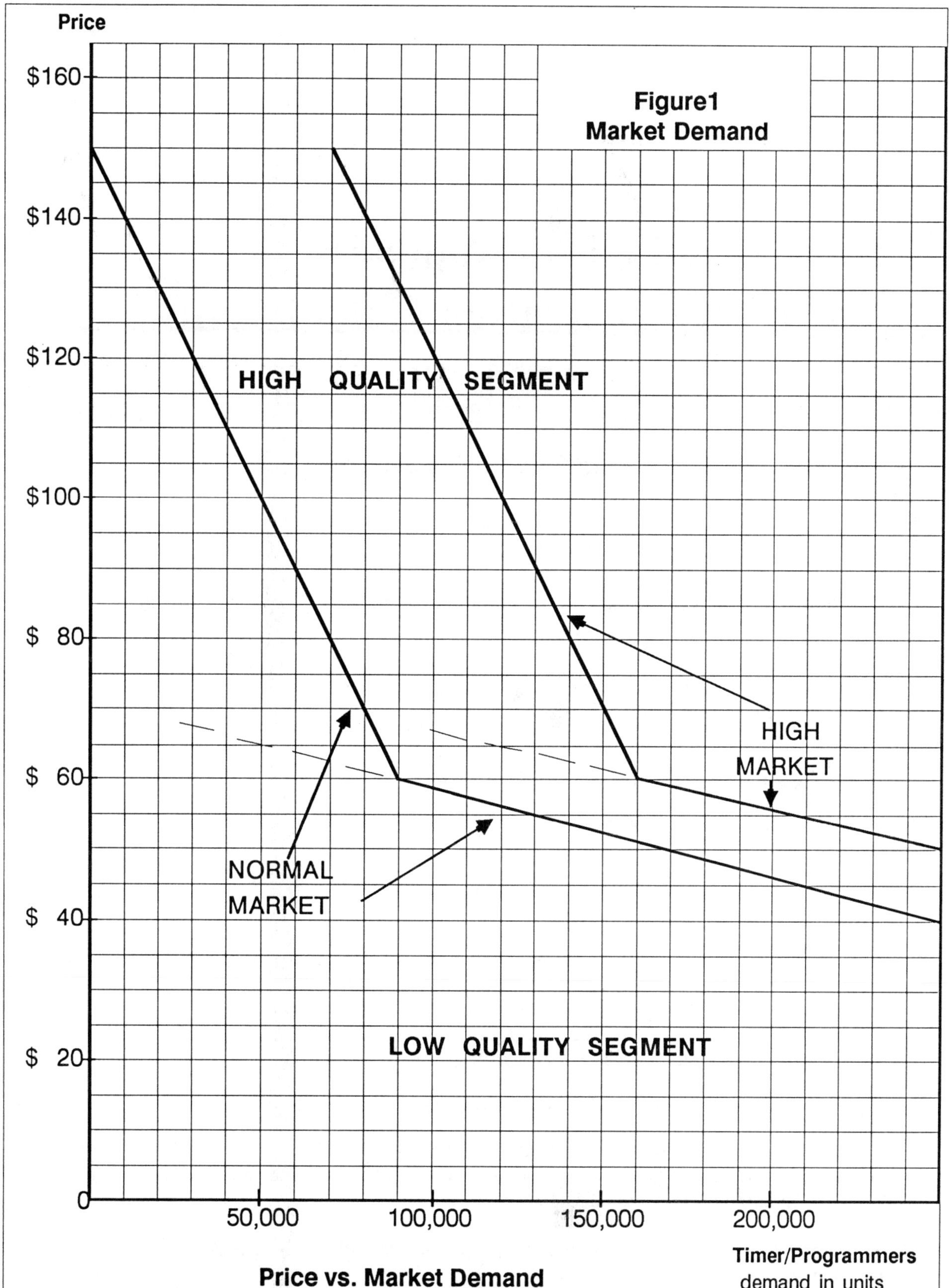

Price vs. Market Demand
with an assumption of $100,000 of effective advertising per segment

PART I — Appendix 1
Market Penetration Calculations

Case 1: One Firm Enters the High Quality Segment

Assumptions

1. Only one firm (say firm A) has set $P_A > \$60$
2. That firm does not have the least RE in both Engineering **and** Design of all the firms.

   Then, firm A has sales quantity

$$Q_A = (150{,}000 - 1000P_A)\frac{[A_A - .3(A_B + A_C)]^{.15}}{(100{,}000)^{.15}}$$

Where A_A is the effective advertising of firm A, etc...

The other firms, B & C, have total sales,

$$Q_{BC} = (510{,}000 - 7000P_{BC})\frac{(A_B + A_C)^{.15}}{(100{,}000)^{.15}} - Q_A \quad [\text{ note}^{5,\,6}]$$

Where $P_{BC} = \dfrac{2P_BP_C}{P_B + P_C}$ (the harmonic mean of prices charged by firm B and firm C)

Then $$Q_B = \frac{[(A_B)^{.3}\, T_B/P_B]}{[(A_B)^{.3}\, T_B/P_B + (A_C)^{.3}\, T_C/P_C]} \times Q_{BC},\text{ where}$$

T_B is the Total Resource Effectiveness of firms B and Q_C = etc. . . .

When only two firms (A and B) remain in CONFRONTATION, and one enters the higher quality segment, Q_B is given above by Q_{BC}. When both enter the lower quality segment, $Q_A = 0$. Q_B and Q_C are calculated as above.

---

5 The subtraction of Q_A is necessary since the buyers in the high price market segment have already been satisfied by firm A.

6 These equations assume a normal-sized market, see the equation on p. 10 for the high market.

Case 2: Two Firms Enter the High Quality Segment

Assumptions

1. Two firms have set P > \$60 (say firms A + B)
2. Neither firm has the lowest RE in both Engineering and Design of the three firms

   If 1 and 2 **both** apply

Then $$Q_{AB} = (150{,}000 - 1000P_{AB})\,\frac{(A_A + A_B - .3A_C)^{.15}}{(100{,}000)^{.15}}$$

Where $$P_{AB} = \frac{2P_BP_A}{P_A + P_B}$$

then $$Q_A = \frac{(A_A)^{.3}\,T_A/P_A \times Q_{AB}}{(A_B)^{.3}\,T_B/P_B + (A_A)^{.3}\,T_A/P_A},$$ and

$$Q_B = \frac{(A_B)^{.3}\,T_B/P_B \times Q_{AB}}{(A_B)^{.3}\,T_B/P_B + (A_A)^{.3}\,T_A/P_A},$$

and $$Q_C = (510{,}000 - 7000P_C)\frac{(A_C)^{.15}}{(100{,}000)^{.15}} - Q_{AB}$$

When only two firms remain in CONFRONTATION, (A and B) $Q_C = 0$

If assumption 1 applies, but 2 does not, then the firm that does **not** have the lowest RE in both Engineering and Design will be treated as if fulfilling the conditions of Case 1. The firm having the lowest RE in Engineering and Design will be treated as if it were in the lower price segment, also as in Case 1.

Case 3: Three Firms Initially Enter the High Quality Segment One is Demoted

Assumptions

1. Three firms have set P > \$60
2. One firm has the lowest RE in both Engineering and Design of the three firms (say firm C).

   Then, firms A & B are each treated as if they are fulfilling the conditions of Case 2. Firm C is perceived as being in the lower price segment.

   This case does not apply when only two competing firms remain.

Case 4: Three Firms Compete in the Same Market Segment

For **all** other situations (that do not fit the above cases), the three firms are in the same market segment,

$$P_{ABC} = \frac{3P_AP_BP_C}{P_AP_B + P_BP_C + P_AP_C}$$ (the harmonic mean of prices charged by all three companies)

and $$Q_{ABC} = (150{,}000 - 1000P_{ABC})\frac{(A_A + A_B + A_C)^{.15}}{(100{,}000)^{.15}}$$

for $P_{ABC} > \$60$

or $$Q_{ABC} = (510{,}000 - 7000P_{ABC})\frac{(A_A + A_B + A_C)^{.15}}{(100{,}000)^{.15}}$$

for $P_{ABC} \leq \$60$

and $$Q_A = \frac{(A_A)^{.3}\,T_A/P_A}{(A_A)^{.3}\,T_A/P_A + (A_B)^{.3}\,T_B/P_B + (A_C)^{.3}\,T_C/P_C} \times Q_{ABC} \text{ etc...}$$

Withdrawal Note

If the test market indicates that a firm shall be unable to achieve the minimum order size and it is withdrawn, then the market penetrations for the remaining firms are recalculated with the withdrawn firm excluded. When this situation, takeover, or bankruptcy results in one firm positioning its product in each market segment, then the one in the higher quality segment has sales as shown in case 1; and the firm in the lower quality segment has sales as shown in case 2.

Production Capacity Note

When two or more firms are sharing a market and one or two firms do not have sufficient production capacity to satisfy their total potential sales, the remaining firm(s) will receive those additional sales if their production capacities are sufficient. When two firms are sharing this extra revenue, the additional unit sales each will receive will be in proportion to their relative market penetration.

PART I — Appendix 2
Confrontation Parameters

MAX PRICE = $180

CONFRONTATION PARAMETERS (Supplied by the Simulation Instructor)

a. $ 5.7 million starting capital.

b. 7 % interest rate on debt.

c. 300 000 shares may be issued at one time (beginning with the third year).

d. $ 350 000 minimum overhead allocation to a department (except General and Administration).

e. 60 % greater cost for raw materials in excess of planned production.

f. 15 % is the minimum raw material cost as a % of selling price.

g. 270 % of inventory's balance sheet value is the maximum price for which it may be sold.

h. 60 % is income tax rate on profits in excess of $1,000,000.

i. 4 % expected return on the low risk investment.

j. 2 % (percentage points) standard deviation of return.

k. 10 % expected return on the high risk investment.

l. 12 % (percentage points) standard deviation of return.

m. 350 % asset ratio between firms to allow a takeover.

PROFIT SHARING

not on course

____ % to the president when your firm is profitable.

____ % to the manager with largest resource effectiveness.

____ % to the analysis group when your firm's profit is the largest among the three firms.

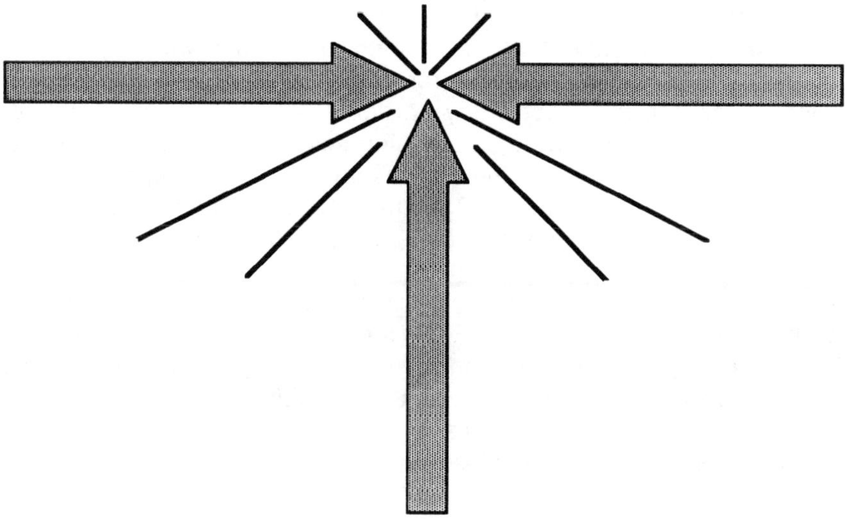

PART II – STRATEGIC PLANNING

15. THE PLANNING PROCESS

The firm that formulates its strategy in a way that is clearly superior to its competitors throughout the simulation will almost always win. Formulating an optimal strategic plan is the central challenge of CONFRONTATION. Your company's strategy will be implemented in about 16 key decisions that are identified on the sample decision sheet. However, each decision can take many values. This results in literally hundreds of thousands of different strategies from which the best plan must be selected. The key to a correct strategic choice is a qualitative and quantitative planning process that efficiently and rigorously examines the range of alternatives.

Although development of the planning process is part of the learning experience offered by the simulation, the broad guidelines that follow may at least suggest an overall planning framework that may be useful. This will introduce the first of two important concepts in planning—a systematic method. Random planning activity is similar to buying a lottery ticket. Once in a very long while it might pay off by sheer accident. This simulation is not likely to last that long. Secondly, the activities of all participants must be coordinated. With five to eight managers working in a well-thought out planning relationship, your firm will have already achieved valuable synergy in the use of its human resources.

Because this manual provides all the relationships between strategic decisions and performance results in quantitative terms, it may be tempting to try to duplicate those algorithms in a personal program, perhaps with spreadsheet software, and attempt to try all possible strategic decision combinations against all possible market situations and competitive strategies. If that were possible, then trial and error would eventually provide a perfect strategy. But beware. It is definitely **not possible**. There are about 10^{13} scenarios to evaluate, well beyond the capability of even the most automated system of trial and error planning. The only way to compete successfully in CONFRONTATION is to preselect a tiny portion of all possible situations for quantitative analysis through a sound qualitative strategic planning sequence that begins with a rigorous environmental evaluation, continues with an internal resource assessment, and concludes with the selection of an appropriate generic strategy. Only then, are quantitative techniques useful to fine tune your firm's strategy and fill in details employing a quantitative analysis.

From the viewpoint of serveral years, planning goes through three phases. Phase 1 takes place prior to the first year's product introduction. Each firm is starting up, without experience in the market place. There is no prior knowledge concerning the likely behaviour of competitors. (Part III provides a complete description of the information available during and after each product introduction.) Typically, caution is used at this stage. Occasionally, a more radical but well-thought out strategy may succeed. It is a riskier approach.

In the second phase, perhaps the second and third years, the behaviour of both competitors and how the market responds becomes better understood. Perhaps no firm has yet gained a substantial advantage in resources. The more accurate and complete analysis and the better planning that can and should take place at this stage will facilitate obtaining ultimate success.

Finally, during the latter half of the simulation, there will almost certainly be substantial differences in the prospects for each firm. Three years or more of operations will have unhinged the initial balance. From the history of prior behaviour and by knowledge of the resources and synergy possessed by each firm, it may be easier to predict the strategic choices that are likely to be made by your competitors. As prediction accuracy increases, however, it is even more important to perform a rigorous analysis of the situation prior to deciding upon a strategic plan. Otherwise the improved accuracy of the information is not being fully utilized.

The planning process that is outlined in Figures 2 and 3 follows a generally accepted framework for strategic planning. The first input is the environmental analysis that includes data from competitors and the market. The market survey can provide the latter information (if it is purchased) while competitive information is chiefly available from the current resource situation and their historical behaviour patterns. When a competitor is suffering from a severe lack of resources, previously observed behaviour may not be representative. Firms with barely adequate resources to enter the market will likely perceive fewer strategic options. Similarly, large inventories may constrain prices that can be set, and low resource effectiveness in engineering and design may force a firm into entering the lower quality market segment.

The second group of inputs to strategic planning is internal to the organization. It includes an assessment of available resources and this assessment can influence the strategic choices that are viable. For example, if your firm withdrew from the market during the previous year, its current advertizing effectiveness will be depressed, its experiential increase in production capacity may be less as compared to competitors, and it will have just suffered a substantial loss in income and share value.

Also encompassed within these internal inputs is management preference. This refers to the generic competitive attitude and the economic values held by your management group. Common generic preferences include:

1. *Maximize Gain*
   Plan to maximize net income (and earnings per share) even in the face of substantial risk.

2. *Minimize Loss*
   Plan to follow conservative low risk strategies to limit the possibility of substantial loss.

3. *Maximize Damage*
   Seek to inflict the maximum loss on competitors, even while sustaining a possible significant loss for your own company.

The above choices refer to the risk preference and attitude towards the competitive situation that your firm wishes to adopt. Within each year select a focus, differentiation, or price leadership strategy as described in Part I.

These generic preferences and similar values will program the strategic function. That is, they should cause management to prefer strategic approaches that are likely to produce outcomes reflecting these values. First, these values are expressed in the Mission statement (see Part III below). That expression seeks to establish the flavour or general direction of company's strategy.

Your firm's resources and the management preference are combined with the environmental analysis to form the information for a set of goals and strategic decisions. These decisions are then tested over a range of possible competitive strategies and synergies by economic scenarios (see below) until particular sets of your strategic decisions produce excellent or best possible results for corresponding sets of likely decisions by competitors. Ultimately, it will be necessary to choose one set of decisions that appear to offer a good prospect for performance over a fair range of possible competitive behaviour.

16. A DETAILED GUIDELINE FOR STRATEGIC PLANNING —See Figure 2

Following the strategic planning sequence outlined below is certainly not the only method available, but it will facilitate a careful examination of strategic alternatives in order to select an appropriate strategy for your company. The following sequence should be undertaken after your corporate mission has been established; and the risk preference, strategic attitude and generic competitive strategy has been provisionally settled.

A. Planning must start somewhere. A logical starting place is the environmental factors that no firm can control. Using market data, evidence of prior competitive behaviour (if any), and knowledge of their resources (and likely synergies), project a possible product price for each competitor.

B. For each product price, a range of competitors' investment (budgetary allocation) behaviour is possible. Initially one set is chosen. Later on, variations must also be considered to more fully test your strategy.

C. Based upon the information and assumptions of Steps A and B, and an assessment of internal resources and management preference, formulate a set of strategic decisions for your company that you believe will meet with success. (See the Economic Scenario Worksheet at the back of this manual.)

D. The synergy factors estimated for the prior steps are predictable only as to their likely or expected value. Calculate a range of outcomes assuming that competitive decisions are as predicted, but with synergy for all firms that varies over a range of possible values.

E. Decide whether the range of possible performance outcomes projected in D are acceptable. Their acceptability will depend upon risk preference and preselected generic strategies such as: maximize gain, minimize potential loss, etc. . . .

F. If the range of outcomes is **not** acceptable, then diagnose the reason and substantially adjust the decisions made in Step C.

G. If the range of performance outcomes is at least minimally acceptable, decide whether it is the best obtainable—again in respect of predetermined management preference.

H. If the range of outcomes is acceptable, but performance could probably be improved, then slightly alter the decisions made in Step C and check for improvement.

I. When projected performance is judged to be the best obtainable, record the match between competitors' strategies and the appropriate strategic response.

J. Have all major competitors' strategies been assessed for a particular selection of market segment and price decisions? If not, return to Step B for a new set.

K. Have all competitors' market segment and price decisions been considered? If no, return to Step A for a new set.

L. When the answers to Steps J and K are both yes, then a set of strategic responses to competitors' strategies has been devised. Then, proceed to Figure 3 for Market Survey Decision.

Note that to complete all of the above steps with every conceivable small and large change in all parameters, even within the bounds of predetermined preferences, would be an impossibly long task. Developing an effective method of formulating and testing these alternative scenarios is one of the challenges of CONFRONTATION. The number of cases to be considered must be limited in a way that does not compromise a thorough examination of possible strategic alternatives. The importance of this limiting procedure is underlined by the fact that after each year of operation, many of the parameters will have changed and therefore the entire analysis will require revamping.

17. THE MARKET SURVEY DECISION—See Figure 3

Steps A to E in Figure 3 illustrate how to decide whether to purchase consultant services in order to survey the market. Since the cost of a survey is $200,000, it should only be purchased if it is expected that having better information regarding the market size will be worth $200,000 or more. Obviously, a firm must be ready to pursue a different strategy depending upon the survey's prediction. A survey that would prompt no strategic change, regardless of its prediction, is clearly of no value. When a market survey is not obtained, the lower probability of a higher volume market occurring would seem to suggest that firms should plan for a normal volume market.

The result of following the procedures of Figure 2 is a series of appropriate strategic responses to possible competitive actions. In each case, it must be decided (as illustrated in Figure 3) whether the market consultant should be hired.

18. SELECTION OF A STRATEGY

The analyses suggested in A Guideline for Planning and The Market Survey Decision above do not in themselves select the optimal strategy. Rather, they disclose a series of appropriate strategic responses in keeping with environmental determinants, resource competence, and management preference. In order to select one strategy, it is necessary to devise a procedure such as that which follows.

A. From all the competitors' strategies considered, select all those that are considered most likely.

B. Choose an internal strategy that best reflects management preference across the range of most likely competitors' strategies.

C. Consider less likely but still possible competitors' strategies. Assess whether the Strategic Decisions selected in B will produce unacceptable results in this instance. If this is the case, then it may be advisable to choose a strategy that does not have this drawback.

The prediction of likely competitors' strategies is difficult for the first year's product introduction. There is generally, among all firms, unfamiliarity with the environment and the use of company resources. As mentioned above, each firm is in a start up condition. The rate of new business failures during recent years attests to the difficulty of succeeding in a new venture. As the simulation proceeds, however, the quantity and quality of useful knowledge, and the ability to use that knowledge will improve dramatically. Of prime importance is the knowledge concerning patterns of competitors' behaviour.

In view of the above, it may be tempting to carry out a rather superficial planning process for the first year's product introduction. This would be a serious error. By the time a firm that follows this procedure is comfortable with the planning process, there may already be a sizeable difference between its resources and those of its harder-working competitors. The best planning possible may not then overcome the disadvantage of a large differential in resources. The depleted firm may be forced into survival strategies by only the third or fourth year. Note that when new enterprises fail, it usually occurs within the first few years!

19. THE SEQUENCE OF STRATEGIC DECISIONS

(Use the Economic Scenario Worksheet forms at the back of this manual)

For purposes of detailed planning, it will be noted that certain decisions, once made, restrict or strongly influence choices in other categories. Following is a sequence that may serve as a guideline for making strategic decisions in the appropriate order. It assumes that the economic scenario has already been listed and the nature of your strategic decisions has been chosen.

A. Choose the market segment.

B. Choose product price and quality of raw materials.

C. Allocate budgetary funds to each department including funds for capital expenditures.

D. Allocate advertising budget and decide whether to purchase a market survey.

E. Forecast sales to order raw materials.

F. Determine minimum order size (See Part I, Section 4).

In parallel, but interdependent with these product decisions are the mainly financial determinations that follow.

G. Evaluate the prospects and desirability of taking over a competitor, or alternatively, the danger of bankruptcy or being taken over. (This may influence decisions A – F.)

H. Decide whether it is possible and appropriate to issue more equity.

I. Decide whether it is possible and appropriate to borrow additional funds.

J. Decide whether and in what way to invest surplus cash.

K. Fill out a Cash Budget Work Sheet to determine whether the chosen strategy is financially feasible.

L. Fill out the Strategic Decision Form.

M. Construct a pro forma income statement and balance sheet.

Part III contains a detailed example illustrating and discussing the strategic decisions of a firm and the performance obtained. It is suggested that this section should be reviewed prior to formulating your firm's decisions.

If you have decided to purchase a market survey, you will need to complete two each of the Decision Sheets, Cash Budgets, and Pro Forma Statements. One version of each will be implemented depending on the result of the survey. An illustrative example of a year's operations is given below in Part III—Strategic Inputs and Performance Outputs. Blank forms on tear-out sheets are provided at the back of this manual.

Figure 2
A Guideline for Planning

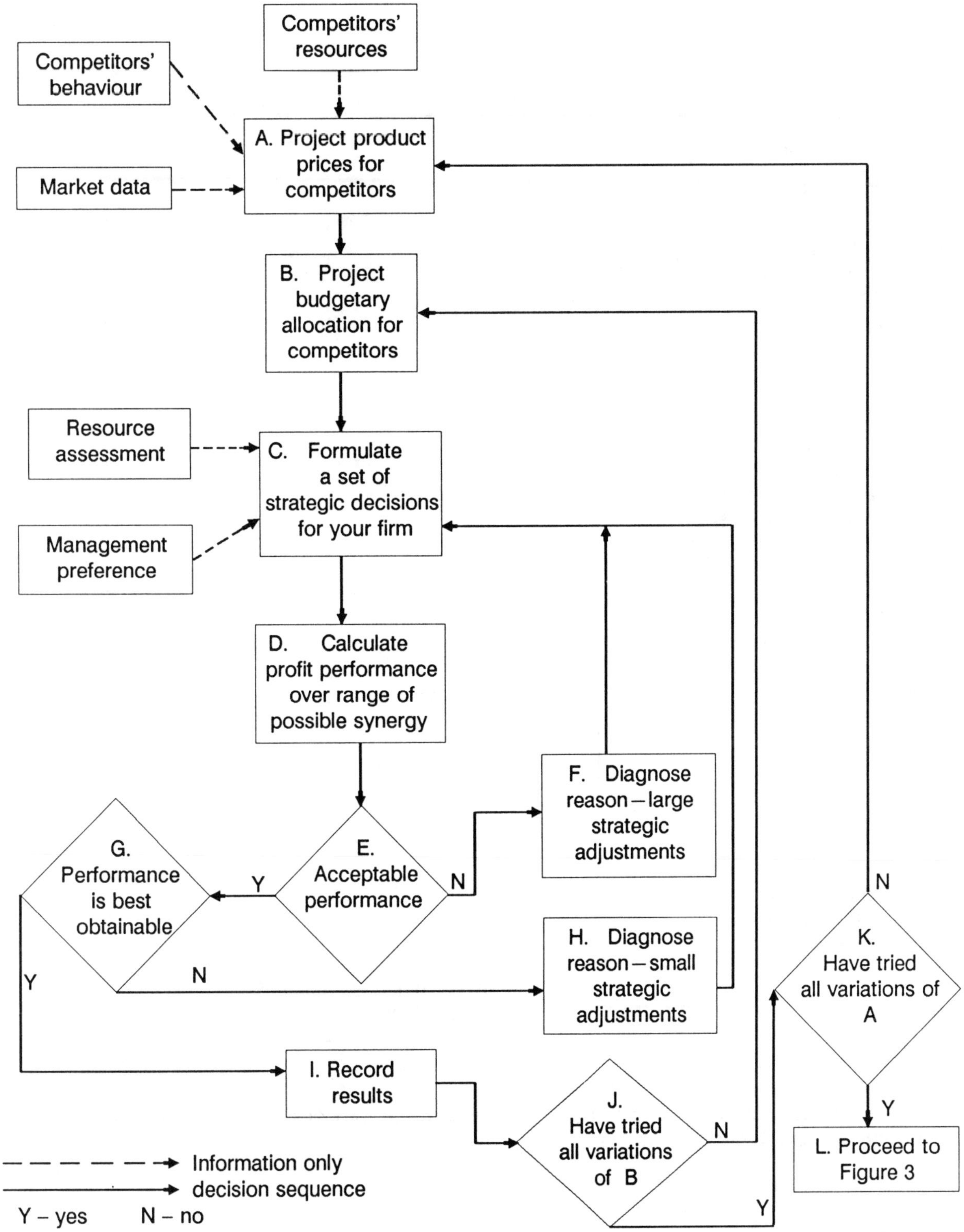

Figure 3
The Market Survey Decision

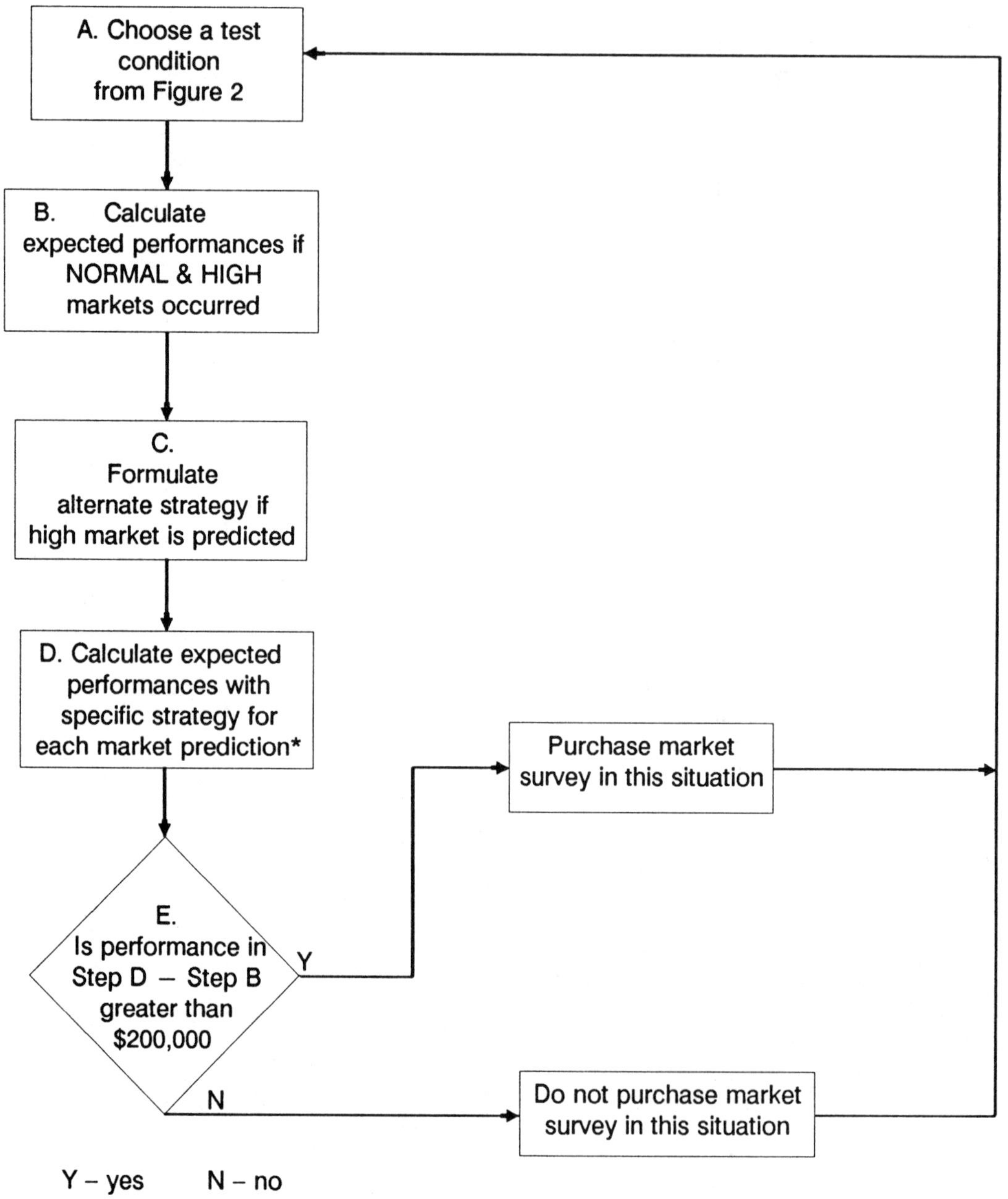

* A rigorous approach requires application of Bayesian probabilities since a survey prediction can still be incorrect.

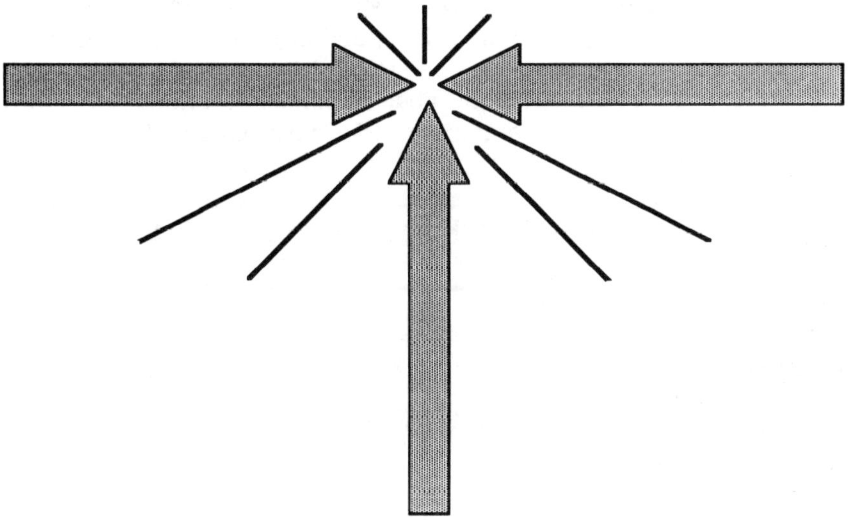

PART III – STRATEGIC INPUTS AND PERFORMANCE OUTPUTS

20. INPUTS

Introduction

In CONFRONTATION, the absence of actual day to day activities enables participants to concentrate upon strategic planning. The elapsed time from when decisions are submitted to the Simulation Instructor to when the results of a whole year's operations are distributed to participants may be only a few minutes. Therefore, this simulation mainly centers upon strategic planning and the evaluation of results obtained. In fact it is the planning process that is intended to be emphasized. The required inputs require extensive analysis of strategic information for their formulation and the outputs are designed to facilitate strategic planning for the following year and beyond.

The submissions described below may help you to establish an orderly planning routine that should aid firms in the formulation of successful strategies.

The General Statement of Strategy

Prior to formulating the set of specific strategic decisions, which is the required input to take part in the simulation, it is necessary to follow the strategic sequence outlined in Figure 2, or a similar one. The method of strategic planning described in Part II is compatible with the following sequence of activities and submissions. The steps of this process will result in the formulation of the General Statement of Strategy that must be submitted prior to the first year's product introduction. This statement, can be separated into four main parts as follows:

A. Determinants of Strategy (See Part II for detailed description)

1. Environmental Assessment (external)
2. Resource Assessment (internal)
3. Statement of Management Values or Preference

The three headings incorporate three bodies of information that determine strategy. In this section, as in the ones to follow, it is important to be as specific and detailed as possible. From time to time Section I will need revision as the simulation progresses, due to changes in the external situation as well as to your firm's resources.

B. The Long Range Plan

1. *Mission*
   Describe the business of the firm in 25 to 40 words. Mention the quality of product, preferred market segment, risk preference, generic strategy, etc.
2. *Long Range Goals*
   Long range goals should not just be the stated desire to win the simulation. They should cover such things as the ultimate market penetration you intend to achieve, the return on investment target, share value objective, takeover goals, etc. . . . These should apply over the entire simulation.
3. *Overall Policies*
   These are general statements of policy that will organize resources to achieve the Long Range Goals. The policies might cover each manager's responsibility in strategic decision-making, their overall coordination, and possibly how strategic planning is to be accomplished. The latter might refer to what planning aids or techniques are intended to be used.
4. *Rationale*
   Within each of the above three headings or under a separate heading, state the reasons you have for selecting this mission, goal, or policy.

Section B will likely require revision during the simulation as CONFRONTATION becomes better known, and as the results of the first few years prompt a reevaluation, upward or downward, of your firm's prospects.

C. The Year's Strategy

1. *Goals*
   Be objective (quantitative) as far as possible with respect to desired attainments. Appropriate objectives might include market penetration, sales, contribution margin, net profit, etc. . . .

2. *Major Policies*
   These should explain how your firm has organized with respect to organizational structure, communication channels and information acquisition, resource allocation, and modes of making decisions.

   The method of assessing competitors' behaviour and resources, and how various strategic alternatives are evaluated should be explained in detail. Use of the Economic Scenario Worksheet, for example, can be described. During the second and subsequent years, the Strategic Control System described in Part IV may be useful for determining how planning may be improved.

For each yearly product introduction, Section C must be revised. Include a document (see Section IV of this manual) that explains how the current year's strategy deals with the diagnosis and correction of strategic errors in the previous year.

D. Implementation

1. List of Strategic Decisions. (See Figure 4 and use forms appended to this text.)

2. Pro forma Income Statement, Balance Sheet, and Cash Budget Work Sheet.

Section D must be newly formulated for each yearly product introduction.

An explanation should be given as to how the list of Strategic Decisions represents the implementation of major policies described in C2.

Jan 22, 1988 Confrontation Year 2

Balance Sheet

Assets	Protime	Techtime	Elektrix
Cash	8,136,020.00	3,229,741.00	5,342,194.00
Inventory	1,671,581.00	2,911,282.00	637,173.00
Capital Equipment	1,760,000.00	1,520,000.00	1,300,000.00
less depreciation	255,200.00	220,400.00	188,499.90
Total Assets	11,312,400.00	7,440,623.00	7,090,867.00
Liabilities	1,000,000.00	2,000,000.00	0.00
Equity			
Common Shares	7,000,000.00	7,000,000.00	7,000,000.00
Retained Earnings	3,312,401.00	1,559,376.00DB	90,866.69
Total	11,312,400.00	7,440,624.00	7,090,866.00

Press return to continue

Jan 22, 1988 Confrontation Year 2

Company Comparisons

Liquidity	Protime	Techtime	Elektrix
Current Ratio	9.8076	3.0705	
Quick Ratio	8.1360	1.6149	
Working Capital	8,807,602.00	4,141,023.00	5,979,367.00
Debt/Equity	0.0884	0.2688	0.0000
Performance			
Operating Margin	0.0956	0.3921DB	0.1434DB
Current R.O.I.	0.0642	0.2164DB	0.0873DB
Avg Earnings/Share	1.66	0.78DB	0.89
Market Price/Share	21.24	0.00	4.35

Personal Accounts

Protime		Techtime		Elektrix	
Mel	196,081.20	Linda	0.00	George	32,271.07
Frank	0.00	Mabel	0.00	Lisa	64,542.15
Jim	0.00	Gordon	0.00	Nancy	0.00
Mary	327,566.10	Hilda	0.00	Alan	0.00
Ann	64,596.56	Peter	0.00	Clement	0.00
Sue	294,122.00	Lily	0.00	Fran	0.00
Art		John		Ivan	
Len				Catherine	

Press return to continue

21. PROTIME'S INPUTS: YEAR 3

An Illustrative Example

PROTIME stated its mission as "domination of the high quality market segment with technically advanced programmer/timers". In fact, they have positioned their products in that segment for two years with relatively good results.

The balance sheet opposite is from the previous year end shows that PROTIME is developing a significant financial advantage over its competitors, TECHTIME and ELEKTRIX. This is best shown by the cash and retained earnings that are substantially better. In fact, TECHTIME's retained earnings are negative (indicated by DB for debit balance). The main potential difficulty for PROTIME seems to be a fairly large inventory. In the high quality segment, it may not be possible to charge a low enough price to enable a company to sell existing inventory (See Part I—Inventory) and remain in the high quality segment. If PROTIME decided instead to enter the low quality segment, it would likely have the disadvantage of competing directly with two firms, and it would lose one-half of its advertising effectiveness carry-over from year two. TECHTIME's inventory is larger, but that company has been concentrating on the low quality market segment, where a price reduction is easier to obtain.

PROTIME's greatest Year 3 advantage is its ability to issue shares at a marginal price of $21.24/share. ELEKTRIX, the closest competitor, is only able to receive a much lower price for its shares. Its prior performance, (and that of TECHTIME) has not produced a financial market perception of a high share value. Normally, the amount of shares a firm may issue is much more limited. In this example, PROTIME could issue any number of shares up to 2,750,000 and chose 2,740,000.

Note: DB means debit balance, a negative number!

Strategic Decision Form

For Year 3

Market Assumption	High / Normal / (No Survey)
Company Name	PROTIME
Year	3RD
President	MEL
Analysts(s)	SUE
	ART
	LEN
Marketing Manager	FRANK
Production Manager	JIM
Engineering Manager	MARY
Design Manager	ANN

FINANCIAL AND PROMOTIONAL DECISIONS

Issue of Shares	# 2,740,000
Increase Loan by $ / or Decrease Loan by	$ 0
Capital Equipment Investment	$ 880,000
Financial Investment / A or B	$ 1,000,000 (/A) or B
Advertising Expenditure	$ 800,000

BUDGETARY ALLOCATIONS

Marketing Department	$ 750,000
Production Department	$ 300,000
Engineering Department	$ 500,000
Design Department	$ 750,000
General and Administration	$ 250,000

SALES AND PRODUCTION DECISIONS

Product Price	$ 65.00
Raw Material Cost	$ 22.00
Minimum Yearly Sales	# 82,000
Production Quantity	# 179,800

Strategic Decision Form

Choosing a price of $65 maintains PROTIME'S strategic mission of attempting to dominate the high quality market segment. That price falls within the segment; but it is close to the low end. It is an attempt to differentiate its product from the competition, but not a focus strategy that would require a much heavier investment in raw materials. This means that should ELEKTRIX enter the high quality segment as well (TECHTIME's severe inventory problem effectively prevents them from doing so), they will not be able to divert market penetration from PROTIME simply due to a lower price. Secondly, PROTIME's substantial advertising expenditure of $1,000,000 is an aggressive expenditure beyond the amount needed to maximize profit, but it is perhaps within the range needed to counter advertising of firms in the lower segment. Finally, substantial budgetary support for the Engineering and Design Departments tries to ensure that the firm's products will not be seen as inferior by the market, which would otherwise effectively demote PROTIME to the low quality segment in the mind of the consumer.

On the negative side, it might be considered whether the sales revenue that could be enjoyed by PROTIME will cover these substantial expenditures. In this year at least, this company may be attempting to dominate the market even at the expense of profits. Offsetting this somewhat risky approach, is the fact that excess working capital has been invested in a relatively risk-free investment—perhaps to counter potential losses. However, when it is considered (see cash budget work sheet and Year 3 balance sheet below) that the firm is counting on raising $23 million via a share offering, the $1,000,000 financial investment seems unnecessarily small. The capital equipment commitment is however, not defensible. PROTIME already has more capital equipment than it needs (see actual production capacity below). Needless amounts of this asset only attracts large depreciation expenses that reduce profitability.

Cash Budget Work Sheet For Year 3

	$	$	
Sources of Cash at Beginning of Year			
Starting Cash	8,136,020		
Proceeds of New Equity Issue	22,640,055		
Loan Capital	0		
Total Cash Sources at Beginning of Year		30,776,075	(1)
Cash Committed at Beginning of Year			
Repayment of Loan	0		
Purchase of Capital Equipment	880,000		
Advertising Expenditure	800,000		
Purchase of Market Survey	0		
Departmental Budgetary Allocations	2,300,000		
General and Administration Allocation	250,000		
External Financial Investment	1,000,000		
Total Cash Committed at Beginning of Year		5,230,000	(2)
Net Cash at Beginning of Year (1) – (2) [(3) Must be a positive number]		25,546,075	(3)
Planned Production x 1/2 Raw Material Cost/Unit [(3) must not be less than (4) if there is a financial investment]		988,900	(4)
Impact of Sales			
Expected Sales Revenue	11,687,000		
less Total Raw Material Expense	1,977,800		
Inventory Expenses	200,590		
Sales Revenue net of Variable Costs		9,508,610	(5)
Expected Revenue from Financial Investment plus Principal		1,060,000	(6)
Net Cash before Tax and Profit Sharing [(3) + (5) + (6)]		36,114,685	(7)
Final Expenditures			
Interest Expense	360,000		
Income Tax	3,379,444		
Estimated Profit sharing	700,000		
Total End of Year Cash Deductions	4,439,444 (8)		
Final Cash Position (7) – (8)		31,675,241	

Cash Budget Work Sheet for PROTIME

The purpose of the Cash Budget Work Sheet is mainly to ensure that the strategic decisions made can be implemented with available funds, and that available funds are being adequately utilized for operations or investment purposes.

1. **Source of Cash at Beginning of Year** reflects the funds available for commitment early in the strategic period. The three sources are working capital, share capital, and debt capital.
2. **Cash Committed at Beginning of Year** includes all planned uses of capital except purchasing raw material (which can be financed through sales revenue).
3. **Net Cash at Beginning of Year** must be a positive amount to take part in the Year's simulation. However, if a financial investment is to be made, then there must be sufficient net cash remaining to cover one half the initial raw material commitment. This is to provide some protection against the investment yielding a negative return, or against an inventory buildup at year end.
4. **Impact of Sales and Investment** estimates the net cash inflow due to operations plus an investment in opportunity A or B. The raw material costs are known precisely unless sales exceeds planned production. Inventory costs would include the expense of storing and then refurbishing or discarding the previous year's inventory. Although PROTIME has budgeted enough for refurbishing, it can be seen below that they in fact had to discard it as a result of the current price being too high to place last year's goods on the market. The assumption that they could sell their inventory could have been checked by multiplying the inventory cost on the balance sheet by 1.75 and dividing that result by the number of units in inventory. If the amount is less than their intended price, all the units in inventory must be discarded.
5. **Year End Expenditures** estimates cash disbursements to profit-sharing, which cannot be accurately predicted, and projects the income tax liability.
6. **Year End Cash Position** is the amount of cash that PROTIME expects to see on its balance sheet at the end of the year.

Note that PROTIME overestimated the proceeds of its equity issue by nearly $8M by inaccurately accounting for the share dilution factor. (See p. 55.)

Jan 22, 1988 Confrontation Year 3

Internal Performance and Market Size

	Protime	Techtime	Elektrix
Total Departmental Allocation	2,300,000.00	1,450,000.00	2,195,000.00
Resource Effectiveness			
Marketing	900,000.00	796,249.60	1,271,874.00
Production	466,137.90	470,717.00	549,590.20
Engineering	427,103.10	161,088.30	260,464.80
Design	336,967.70	229,940.50	325,581.10
Total Resource Effectiveness	2,130,208.70	1,657,995.00	2,407,510.00
Price	65.00	25.00	35.00
Minimum Unit Sales Volume	82,000.00	40,000.00	53,000.00
Planned Production	179,800.00	155,580.00	180,600.00
Production Capacity	422,526.00	313,110.00	424,875.00

The market size is Normal

Press return to continue

22. PROTIME'S OUTPUTS

Marketing Resource Effectiveness

MRE = Marketing Allocation x Synergy Factor

MRE = $750,000 x 1.2 = 900,000

Production Resource Effectiveness

PRE = $[\text{Production Allocation} \times (\text{Net Capital Equipment})^{.6}]^{.6} \times \text{Synergy Factor}$

PRE = $[\$300{,}000 \times (\$2{,}146{,}320)^{.6}]^{.6} \times 1.2672 = 466{,}137.9$

Engineering Resource Effectiveness

ERE = $\text{Engineering Allocation} \times [\text{Raw Material Price/Product Price}]^{.75} \times \text{Synergy Factor}$

ERE = $\$500{,}000 \times [22/65]^{.75} \times 1.925 = 427{,}103.10$

Design Resource Effectiveness

DRE = $\text{Design Allocation} \times [\text{Raw Material Price/Product Price}]^{.75} \times \text{Synergy Factor}$

DRE = $\$750{,}000 \times [22/65]^{.75} \times 1.0125 = 336{,}967.7$

The Total Resource Effectiveness for each company is the sum of Departmental Resource Effectiveness.

The Synergy Factor is the average of the previous year's factor and a new synergy factor selected automatically from the table in Part I, Section 3. For Marketing Resource Effectiveness, the factor for two of the first three years has been 1.7; and 0.7 for the third year. For all of the departments, the factors have changed since the first year, which is the reason they do not now exactly correspond to the random factors given in the previous table.

Jan 22, 1988 Confrontation Year 3

Internal Performance and Market Size

	Protime	Techtime	Elektrix
Total Departmental Allocation	2,300,000.00	1,450,000.00	2,195,000.00
Resource Effectiveness			
Marketing	900,000.00	796,249.60	1,271,874.00
Production	466,137.90	470,717.00	549,590.20
Engineering	427,103.10	161,088.30	260,464.80
Design	336,967.70	229,940.50	325,581.10
Total Resource Effectiveness	2,130,208.70	1,657,995.00	2,407,510.00
Price	65.00	25.00	35.00
Minimum Unit Sales Volume	82,000.00	40,000.00	53,000.00
Planned Production	179,800.00	155,580.00	180,600.00
Production Capacity	422,526.00	313,110.00	424,875.00

The market size is Normal

Press return to continue

Production Capacity

All three firms have production capacities that appear to be in excess of what would be needed, unless one firm was to enter a product with an extremely low price. Otherwise, capital equipment does increase production synergy; but this advantage may be offset by the large depreciation expense that is increased. Production capacity for PROTIME is given by the following equation:

$$.35 \times [(\text{production allocation}) \times (\text{net value of capital equipment})]^{.5} \times \left[\frac{\Sigma Q_i + 100{,}000}{100{,}000}\right]^{.2}$$

Where ΣQ_i is the sum total of PROTIME'S production in years one and two and contributes to the experience factor.

$$.35 \times [300{,}000 \times 2{,}384{,}800]^{.5} \times \left[\frac{492{,}237 + 100{,}000}{100{,}000}\right]^{.2}$$

$$= 422{,}526$$

Note that by the third year, the experience factor accounts for a 43% increase in production capacity. However, the rate of increase levels out sharply in future years due to the exponent value of .2. After a large number of units have been produced, further productivity gains will be minimal.

Jan 22, 1988 Confrontation Year 3

Income Statements

	Protime	Techtime	Elektrix
Unit Sales Volume	101,079.00	143,662.00	193,993.00
$ Sales Volume	6,570,135.00	3,591,550.00	6,789,755.00
Cost of Goods Sold	2,308,064.00	3,154,004.00	2,189,573.00
Gross Margin	4,262,071.00	437,545.20	4,600,181.00
Operating Expenses			
Inventory Storage	200,589.80	582,256.30	76,460.72
Inventory Write Down	1,671,581.00	0.00	637,172.70
Marketing Overhead	750,000.00	650,000.00	925,000.00
Advertising Expenses	800,000.00	415,000.00	1,000,000.00
Production Overhead	150,000.00	130,000.00	205,000.00
Engineering Overhead	500,000.00	270,000.00	430,000.00
Design Overhead	750,000.00	270,000.00	430,000.00
Depreciation	238,479.90	159,960.00	176,150.00
General & Admin Overhead	250,000.00	250,000.00	250,000.00
Interest Expense	120,000.00	240,000.00	0.00
Total Operating Expense	5,430,651.00	2,967,216.00	4,129,783.00
Profit Sharing	0.00	0.00	82,949.78
Profit	1,168,580.00DB	2,529,671.00	387,448.20
Investment Income	88,575.54	0.00	9,565.84DB
Net Profit (before tax)	1,080,004.00DB	2,529,671.00DB	377,882.30
Income Tax	0.00	0.00	0.00
Net Profit (after tax)	1,080,004.00DB	2,529,671.00DB	377,882.30

Press return to continue

Jan 22, 1988 Confrontation Year 3

Balance Sheets

Assets	Protime	Techtime	Elektrix
Cash	21,836,890.00	2,494,975.00	10,048,510.00
Inventory	1,797,535.00	976,337.10	0.00
Capital Equipment	2,640,000.00	1,820,000.00	1,950,000.00
less depreciation	493,680.00	380,360.00	364,649.90
Total Assets	25,780,740.00	4,910,952.00	11,633,860.00
Liabilities	1,000,000.00	2,000,000.00	0.00
Equity			
Common Shares	22,548,340.00	7,000,000.00	11,165,120.00
Retained Earnings	2,232,396.00	4,089,047.00DB	468,748.70
Total	25,780,740.00	4,910,953.00	11,633,860.00

Press return to continue

Income Statement

- Unit Sales Volume and Advertising Effectiveness

By its pricing strategy, PROTIME has positioned its product in the high quality market segment while its two competitors are in the low quality segment. Here, it will be instructive to calculate the sales volume for both PROTIME and one competitor, TECHTIME. First, since it affects sales volume strongly, advertising effectiveness is calculated for PROTIME and given for TECHTIME and ELEKTRIX.

Year 3 Effective Advertising is given by:

$$Y3EA = .65\ Y3A + .35\ [.65(Y2A) + .35 \times .65(Y1A)]$$

where Y1A is the actual advertising expenditure in year one. .65 (Y1A) is effective advertising for year one, and .35 x .65(Y1A) is the amount of year one's effective advertising carried over to year two, etc. . . . (If the company changes market segment, the .35 carry over factor would become .175.) For PROTIME,

$$Y1A = 600{,}000, \quad Y2A = 361{,}375, \quad \text{and } Y3A = 800{,}000$$

$$Y3EA = .65(800{,}000) + .35[.65(361{,}375) + .35 \times .65(600{,}000)]$$

$$Y3EA = 649{,}988$$

Similarly, TECHTIME's and Elektrix's effective advertising are 325,137 and 783,475 respectively.

PROTIME's sales volume, given a normal market is given by:

$$Q_P = [(150{,}000 - 1{,}000P_P)] \times \left[\frac{A_P - .3(A_T + A_E)}{100{,}000}\right]^{.15}$$

$$Q_P = [150{,}000 - (1{,}000 \times 65)] \times \left[\frac{649{,}988 - .3(325{,}137 + 783{,}475)}{100{,}000}\right]^{.15}$$

$$Q_P = 101{,}079 \text{ units}$$

Where Q_P is sales volume, P_P is price and A_P is the amount of effective advertising for PROTIME, etc. . . .

To calculate TECHTIME's sales volume, it is first necessary to calculate the composite price as perceived by the low quality market segment.

$$P_{TE} = \frac{2P_TP_E}{P_T + P_E} = \frac{2 \times 25 \times 35}{25 + 35} = \$\,29.17$$

Jan 22, 1988 Confrontation Year 3

Income Statements

	Protime	Techtime	Elektrix
Unit Sales Volume	101,079.00	143,662.00	193,993.00
$ Sales Volume	6,570,135.00	3,591,550.00	6,789,755.00
Cost of Goods Sold	2,308,064.00	3,154,004.00	2,189,573.00
Gross Margin	4,262,071.00	437,545.20	4,600,181.00
Operating Expenses			
Inventory Storage	200,589.80	582,256.30	76,460.72
Inventory Write Down	1,671,581.00	0.00	637,172.70
Marketing Overhead	750,000.00	650,000.00	925,000.00
Advertising Expenses	800,000.00	415,000.00	1,000,000.00
Production Overhead	150,000.00	130,000.00	205,000.00
Engineering Overhead	500,000.00	270,000.00	430,000.00
Design Overhead	750,000.00	270,000.00	430,000.00
Depreciation	238,479.90	159,960.00	176,150.00
General & Admin Overhead	250,000.00	250,000.00	250,000.00
Interest Expense	120,000.00	240,000.00	0.00
Total Operating Expense	5,430,651.00	2,967,216.00	4,129,783.00
Profit Sharing	0.00	0.00	82,949.78
Profit	1,168,580.00DB	2,529,671.00	387,448.20
Investment Income	88,575.54	0.00	9,565.84DB
Net Profit (before tax)	1,080,004.00DB	2,529,671.00DB	377,882.30
Income Tax	0.00	0.00	0.00
Net Profit (after tax)	1,080,004.00DB	2,529,671.00DB	377,882.30

Press return to continue

Jan 22, 1988 Confrontation Year 3

Balance Sheets

Assets	Protime	Techtime	Elektrix
Cash	21,836,890.00	2,494,975.00	10,048,510.00
Inventory	1,797,535.00	976,337.10	0.00
Capital Equipment	2,640,000.00	1,820,000.00	1,950,000.00
less depreciation	493,680.00	380,360.00	364,649.90
Total Assets	25,780,740.00	4,910,952.00	11,633,860.00
Liabilities	1,000,000.00	2,000,000.00	0.00
Equity			
Common Shares	22,548,340.00	7,000,000.00	11,165,120.00
Retained Earnings	2,232,396.00	4,089,047.00DB	468,748.70
Total	25,780,740.00	4,910,953.00	11,633,860.00

Press return to continue

Then, the quantity sold by TECHTIME and ELEKTRIX is:

$$Q_{TE} = [510{,}000 - 7000\ P_{TE}] \times \left[\frac{A_B + A_C}{100{,}000}\right]^{.15} - Q_A$$

$$= [510{,}000 - 7000(29.17)] \times \left[\frac{325{,}137 + 783{,}475}{100{,}000}\right]^{.15} - 101{,}079$$

$$Q_{TE} = 337{,}655 \text{ units}$$

TECHTIME's market share and quantity sold is expressed by:

$$Q_T = \frac{(A_T)^{.3} \times T_T/P_T}{(A_T)^{.3} \times T_T/P_T + (A_E)^{.3} \times T_E/P_E} \times Q_{TE}$$

Where T_T is TECHTIME's Total Resource Effectiveness

$$Q_T = \frac{(325{,}137)^{.3} \times (1{,}657{,}995/25)}{(325{,}137)^{.3} \times (1{,}657{,}995/25) + (783{,}475)^{.3} \times (2{,}407{,}510/35)} \times 337{,}655$$

$$Q_T = 143{,}662 \text{ units}$$

- Cost of Goods Sold for PROTIME and TECHTIME

PROTIME's Cost of Goods Sold is calculated as follows:

$$COGS_P = [Q_P \times R_P] + \left[\frac{\text{Production Allocation}}{2} \times \frac{\text{Sales}}{\text{Actual Production}}\right]$$

Where Rp is PROTIME's unit raw material cost. The last term in the brackets accounts for the fact that some of the current production, 78,721 units, went into inventory.

$$COSG_P = [101{,}079 \times 22] + \left[\frac{(300{,}000)}{2} \times \frac{(101{,}079)}{179{,}800}\right]$$

$$= \$\ 2{,}308{,}064$$

In the case of TECHTIME, however, it is first necessary to account for inventory sold as it was not discarded.

New Production sold for TECHTIME is given by:

Year 3 Quantity Sold (Q_T)	143,662
less Year 2 Ending Inventory (units)	– 112,685
New Production Sold (NQ_T)	30,977

Jan 22, 1988 Confrontation Year 3

Income Statements

	Protime	Techtime	Elektrix
Unit Sales Volume	101,079.00	143,662.00	193,993.00
$ Sales Volume	6,570,135.00	3,591,550.00	6,789,755.00
Cost of Goods Sold	2,308,064.00	3,154,004.00	2,189,573.00
Gross Margin	4,262,071.00	437,545.20	4,600,181.00
Operating Expenses			
Inventory Storage	200,589.80	582,256.30	76,460.72
Inventory Write Down	1,671,581.00	0.00	637,172.70
Marketing Overhead	750,000.00	650,000.00	925,000.00
Advertising Expenses	800,000.00	415,000.00	1,000,000.00
Production Overhead	150,000.00	130,000.00	205,000.00
Engineering Overhead	500,000.00	270,000.00	430,000.00
Design Overhead	750,000.00	270,000.00	430,000.00
Depreciation	238,479.90	159,960.00	176,150.00
General & Admin Overhead	250,000.00	250,000.00	250,000.00
Interest Expense	120,000.00	240,000.00	0.00
Total Operating Expense	5,430,651.00	2,967,216.00	4,129,783.00
Profit Sharing	0.00	0.00	82,949.78
Profit	1,168,580.00DB	2,529,671.00	387,448.20
Investment Income	88,575.54	0.00	9,565.84DB
Net Profit (before tax)	1,080,004.00DB	2,529,671.00DB	377,882.30
Income Tax	0.00	0.00	0.00
Net Profit (after tax)	1,080,004.00DB	2,529,671.00DB	377,882.30

Press return to continue

Jan 22, 1988 Confrontation Year 3

Balance Sheets

Assets	Protime	Techtime	Elektrix
Cash	21,836,890.00	2,494,975.00	10,048,510.00
Inventory	1,797,535.00	976,337.10	0.00
Capital Equipment	2,640,000.00	1,820,000.00	1,950,000.00
less depreciation	493,680.00	380,360.00	364,649.90
Total Assets	25,780,740.00	4,910,952.00	11,633,860.00
Liabilities	1,000,000.00	2,000,000.00	0.00
Equity			
Common Shares	22,548,340.00	7,000,000.00	11,165,120.00
Retained Earnings	2,232,396.00	4,089,047.00DB	468,748.70
Total	25,780,740.00	4,910,953.00	11,633,860.00

Press return to continue

The remainder of the new production formed the Year 3 ending inventory.

Then TECHTIME's COGS is

$$COGS_T = [NQ_T \times R_P] + \left[\frac{\text{Prorated Production Allocation}}{2}\right] + (\text{Year 2 Inventory Sold})$$

$$COGS_T = [30{,}977 \times 7] + \left[\frac{130{,}000}{2} \times \frac{30{,}977}{155{,}580}\right] + (2{,}911{,}282)$$

$$COGS_T = \$\ 3{,}154{,}004$$

Where Prorated Production Allocation is the portion allocated to Year 3 **sales** as compared to Year 3 ending inventory which is capitalized and appears on the Year 3 balance sheet.

- ## Inventory Storage and Write Down for PROTIME and TECHTIME

Inventory Storage expense for PROTIME does not include a refurbishing charge since all the inventory was discarded.

Storage Expense = .12 x opening inventory
= .12 x 1,671,581
Storage Expense = $ 200,589.80

Inventory writedown is the total amount of inventory, $1,671,581, that was expensed in Year 3.

Inventory Storage Expense for TECHTIME is 20% of the opening inventory, since refurbishing was required.

Storage Expense = .2 x opening inventory
= .2 x 2,911,282
Storage Expense = $ 582,256

- ## Production Overhead

This is simply the amount of this departmental allocation not attached to COGS.

- ## Depreciation

This expense is 10% of the Year 2 ending capital equipment balance.

Jan 22, 1988 Confrontation Year 3

Income Statements

	Protime	Techtime	Elektrix
Unit Sales Volume	101,079.00	143,662.00	193,993.00
$ Sales Volume	6,570,135.00	3,591,550.00	6,789,755.00
Cost of Goods Sold	2,308,064.00	3,154,004.00	2,189,573.00
Gross Margin	4,262,071.00	437,545.20	4,600,181.00
Operating Expenses			
Inventory Storage	200,589.80	582,256.30	76,460.72
Inventory Write Down	1,671,581.00	0.00	637,172.70
Marketing Overhead	750,000.00	650,000.00	925,000.00
Advertising Expenses	800,000.00	415,000.00	1,000,000.00
Production Overhead	150,000.00	130,000.00	205,000.00
Engineering Overhead	500,000.00	270,000.00	430,000.00
Design Overhead	750,000.00	270,000.00	430,000.00
Depreciation	238,479.90	159,960.00	176,150.00
General & Admin Overhead	250,000.00	250,000.00	250,000.00
Interest Expense	120,000.00	240,000.00	0.00
Total Operating Expense	5,430,651.00	2,967,216.00	4,129,783.00
Profit Sharing	0.00	0.00	82,949.78
Profit	1,168,580.00DB	2,529,671.00	387,448.20
Investment Income	88,575.54	0.00	9,565.84DB
Net Profit (before tax)	1,080,004.00DB	2,529,671.00DB	377,882.30
Income Tax	0.00	0.00	0.00
Net Profit (after tax)	1,080,004.00DB	2,529,671.00DB	377,882.30

Press return to continue

Jan 22, 1988 Confrontation Year 3

Balance Sheets

Assets	Protime	Techtime	Elektrix
Cash	21,836,890.00	2,494,975.00	10,048,510.00
Inventory	1,797,535.00	976,337.10	0.00
Capital Equipment	2,640,000.00	1,820,000.00	1,950,000.00
less depreciation	493,680.00	380,360.00	364,649.90
Total Assets	25,780,740.00	4,910,952.00	11,633,860.00
Liabilities	1,000,000.00	2,000,000.00	0.00
Equity			
Common Shares	22,548,340.00	7,000,000.00	11,165,120.00
Retained Earnings	2,232,396.00	4,089,047.00DB	468,748.70
Total	25,780,740.00	4,910,953.00	11,633,860.00

Press return to continue

- Profit Sharing for ELEKTRIX

The only company to be profitable in the third year, ELEKTRIX's profit sharing can be calculated as follows:

President (George)
$460,832 x .04 = $18,433.29

Manager with highest Resource Effectiveness (Lisa—Marketing)
$460,832.16 x .08 = $36,866.57

Analyst when ELEKTRIX's net profit is highest (Fran)
$460,832.16 x 0.06 = $27,649.93

$460,832 is the net income before tax and profit sharing, but including investment income.

- Investment Income for PROTIME

PROTIME decided to invest $1,000,000 in investment A and received an 8.8% return. This is within one standard deviation (4 percentage points) of the mean (6% return). Note that ELEKTRIX suffered a negative return for its investment in Opportunity B.

Balance Sheet

- Cash Balance of PROTIME

Cash was increased first by a substantial equity issue, the proceeds of which are given by:

$$\text{Proceeds of Equity Issue} = \text{\# of new shares x price per share x } \frac{\text{old total of shares}}{\text{new total of shares}}$$

$$= 2{,}740{,}000 \text{ x } 21.24 \text{ x } \frac{1{,}000{,}000}{3{,}740{,}000}$$

Proceeds of Equity Issue = $ 15,560,855 (actual proceeds can differ by up to 0.1%)

Note that although the marginal market price per share in Year 2 was $21.24. The average price received was about $5.68 per share due to the dilution effect of the excessive number sold.

Jan 22, 1988 Confrontation Year 3

Balance Sheets

	Protime	Techtime	Elektrix
Assets			
Cash	21,836,890.00	2,494,975.00	10,048,510.00
Inventory	1,797,535.00	976,337.10	0.00
Capital Equipment	2,640,000.00	1,820,000.00	1,950,000.00
less depreciation	493,680.00	380,360.00	364,649.90
Total Assets	25,780,740.00	4,910,952.00	11,633,860.00
Liabilities	1,000,000.00	2,000,000.00	0.00
Equity			
Common Shares	22,548,340.00	7,000,000.00	11,165,120.00
Retained Earnings	2,232,396.00	4,089,047.00DB	468,748.70
Total	25,780,740.00	4,910,953.00	11,633,860.00

Press return to continue

Jan 22, 1988 Confrontation Year 3

Company Comparisons

	Protime	Techtime	Elektrix
Liquidity			
Current Ratio	23.6344	1.7357	
Quick Ratio	21.8369	1.2475	
Working Capital	22,634,420.00	1,471,312.00	10,048,510.00
Debt/Equity	0.0388	0.4073	0.0000
Performance			
Operating Margin	0.1779DB	0.7043DB	0.0571
Current R.O.I	0.0436DB	0.8690DB	0.0325
Avg Earnings/Share	1.01	1.08DB	0.11
Market Price/Share	5.77	0.00	0.00

Personal Accounts

Protime		Techtime		Elektrix	
Mel	196,081.20	Linda	0.00	George	50,704.35
Frank	0.00	Mabel	0.00	Lisa	101,408.70
Jim	0.00	Gordon	0.00	Nancy	0.00
Mary	327,566.10	Hilda	0.00	Alan	0.00
Ann	64,596.56	Peter	0.00	Clement	0.00
Sue	294,122.00	Lily	0.00	Fran	27,649.93
Art		John		Ivan	
Len				Catherine	

Press return to continue

Cash Sources in Year 3	
Starting Cash (Year 2 Balance Sheet)	$ 8,136,020
Equity Issue	15,560,855
	23,696,875
Cash Uses Year 3	
Net Loss	(1,080,004)
adjustments to net loss	
writedown of Year 2 Inventory (not a cash charge in Year 3)	1,671,581
Year 3 Depreciation (not a cash charge)	238,480
Year 3 Ending Inventory (a cash charge in Year 3)	(1,797,535)
Capital Equipment Purchase	(880,000)
	(1,847,478)
Ending Cash Year 3 (discrepancy due to slightly lower actual proceeds of equity issue)	$21,849,397

It should be noted that the ending cash for Year 3 is substantially less than the company had predicted on the Cash Budget Work Sheet. The firm overestimated the proceeds of its equity issue and did not predict the substantial loss on operations that occurred.

- Change in Equity for PROTIME

The total equity is substantially higher due to the successful share issue at the beginning of year 3. However, the substantial loss of $1,080,004, has decreased the retained earnings by exactly that amount.

Liquidity and Performance Measures

Liquidity Measures for PROTIME

The Current ratio is measured by:

$$\frac{\text{Cash + Inventory}}{\text{Bank Loan (Liabilities)}} = 23.6344$$

The Quick Ratio is the same measurement with inventory not included.

When these ratios are substantially above 1, they are a possible indication of financial health.

Working Capital is given by:

Cash + Inventory – Liabilities = $22,634,420

Jan 22, 1988 Confrontation Year 3

Company Comparisons

	Protime	Techtime	Elektrix
Liquidity			
Current Ratio	23.6344	1.7357	
Quick Ratio	21.8369	1.2475	
Working Capital	22,634,420.00	1,471,312.00	10,048,510.00
Debt/Equity	0.0388	0.4073	0.0000
Performance			
Operating Margin	0.1779DB	0.7043DB	0.0571
Current R.O.I	0.0436DB	0.8690DB	0.0325
Avg Earnings/Share	1.01	1.08DB	0.11
Market Price/Share	5.77	0.00	0.00

Personal Accounts

Protime		Techtime		Elektrix	
Mel	196,081.20	Linda	0.00	George	50,704.35
Frank	0.00	Mabel	0.00	Lisa	101,408.70
Jim	0.00	Gordon	0.00	Nancy	0.00
Mary	327,566.10	Hilda	0.00	Alan	0.00
Ann	64,596.56	Peter	0.00	Clement	0.00
Sue	294,122.00	Lily	0.00	Fran	27,649.93
Art		John		Ivan	
Len				Catherine	

Press return to continue

Working capital includes inventory which, as can be seen from the income statement where PROTIME'S inventory was written off, may not be useful as working capital. The bank indebtedness, while technically short term, is unlikely to require immediate repayment. It may almost be disregarded as limiting working capital unless the firm is in financial difficulty. PROTIME has gained sufficient cash from the equity issue for any immediate use.

Debt-Equity Ratio is given by:

$$\frac{\text{Liabilities}}{\text{Total Assets}} = .0388$$

This indicates that PROTIME's current borrowing power is substantial, since it may take on debt up to a ratio of .40.

• Performance Measures for PROTIME

Operating margin is negative due to the loss. It is measured by:

$$\frac{\text{Net Profit} - \text{Investment Income} - \text{Profit Sharing}}{\text{Sales}}$$

$$\text{Operating Margin} = \frac{(-1{,}080{,}004) - 88{,}575.54}{6{,}570{,}135} = -.1779$$

Return on investment (ROI), also negative, is calculated as:

$$\frac{\text{Net profit}}{\text{Total Assets}} = \frac{-1{,}080{,}004}{25{,}780{,}740}$$

$$\text{ROI} = -.0436$$

Average Earnings per share is the mean of the yearly earnings per share, for each year of PROTIME's operation. Since the company has been operating for three years, this quantity can be calculated as follows:

$$\left[\frac{\text{Y1 net income}}{1{,}000{,}000\text{ shares}} + \frac{\text{Y2 net income}}{1{,}000{,}000\text{ shares}} + \frac{\text{Y3 net income}}{3{,}740{,}000\text{ shares}}\right] \div 3$$

$$\overline{\text{EPS}} = \left[\frac{2{,}650{,}287}{1{,}000{,}000} + \frac{662{,}115}{1{,}000{,}000} + \frac{(-1{,}080{,}004)}{3{,}740{,}000}\right] \div 3$$

$$\overline{\text{EPS}} = \$\ 1.01$$

Market Price per share is calculated from Average Earnings per share where:

Net Price per share = 8 [2.2 x Avg EPS) – VAR]

VAR is the variance in the year to year earnings given by:

$$\text{VAR} = \frac{(\text{EPS Y1} - \text{AVG EPS})^2}{3} + \frac{(\text{EPS Y2} - \text{AVG EPS})^2}{3} + \frac{(\text{EPS Y3} - \text{Avg EPS})^2}{3}$$

Jan 22, 1988 Confrontation Year 3

Company Comparisons

Liquidity	Protime	Techtime	Elektrix
Current Ratio	23.6344	1.7357	
Quick Ratio	21.8369	1.2475	
Working Capital	22,634,420.00	1,471,312.00	10,048,510.00
Debt/Equity	0.0388	0.4073	0.0000
Performance			
Operating Margin	0.1779DB	0.7043DB	0.0571
Current R.O.I	0.0436DB	0.8690DB	0.0325
Avg Earnings/Share	1.01	1.08DB	0.11
Market Price/Share	5.77	0.00	0.00

Personal Accounts

Protime		Techtime		Elektrix	
Mel	196,081.20	Linda	0.00	George	50,704.35
Frank	0.00	Mabel	0.00	Lisa	101,408.70
Jim	0.00	Gordon	0.00	Nancy	0.00
Mary	327,566.10	Hilda	0.00	Alan	0.00
Ann	64,596.56	Peter	0.00	Clement	0.00
Sue	294,122.00	Lily	0.00	Fran	27,649.93
Art		John		Ivan	
Len				Catherine	

Press return to continue

Jan 22, 1988 Confrontation After Year 3 Takeover

Balance Sheets

Assets	Protime	Techtime	Elektrix
Cash	21,775,828.64	0.00	10,048,510.00
Inventory	1,797,535.00	0.00	0.00
Capital Equipment	4,460,000.00	0.00	1,950,000.00
less depreciation	874,040.00	0.00	364,649.90
Total Assets	27,159,323.64	0.00	11,633,860.00
Liabilities	3,000,000.00	0.00	0.00
Equity			
Common Shares	22,548,340.00	0.00	11,165,120.00
Retained Earnings	1,610,983,64	0.00	468,748.70
Total	27,159,323.64	0.00	11,633,860.00

Press return to continue

$$= \frac{(2.65 - 1.01)^2}{3} + \frac{(.662 - 1.01)^2}{3} + \frac{(-.29 - 1.01)^2}{3}$$

VAR = 1.500

Market Price per share = 8[(2.2 x 1.01) − 1.500]

Market Price per share = $ 5.78

The shares now have much less value. The chief reason for this is the significant loss suffered in year 3 by PROTIME, which would cause investors to worry about that company's financial future.

23. TAKEOVER! ! !

PROTIME's Balance Sheet After Takeover

- Cash

PROTIME's cash is increased by that of the firm it has taken over, TECHTIME, and by the disposal of the latter firm's inventory for between 30¢ and 60¢ on the dollar. (In this case the random variable was 40¢.) Cash is decreased by the requirement to pay the acquired company's shareholders 60% of total asset value. The cash balance on the after takeover Balance Sheet is given by: (See also Year 3 (Y3) balance sheet)

	Cash of PROTIME at end of Y3	$ 21,836,890.00
+	Cash of TECHTIME at end of Y3	+ 2,494,975.00
+	.40 x (TECHTIME's inventory)	+ 390,534.84
−	.60 x (TECHTIME's total assets)	− 2,946,571.20
=	Cash of PROTIME after takeover	$ 21,775,828.64

- Inventory

Since TECHTIME's inventory has been sold, the balance sheet item is PROTIME's ending inventory.

- Capital Equipment and Depreciation

These items are the sum of PROTIME'S and TECHTIME's Y3 balance sheet entries.

Jan 22, 1988 Confrontation After Year 3 Takeover

Balance Sheets

	Protime	Techtime	Elektrix
Assets			
Cash	21,775,828.64	0.00	10,048,510.00
Inventory	1,797,535.00	0.00	0.00
Capital Equipment	4,460,000.00	0.00	1,950,000.00
less depreciation	874,040.00	0.00	364,649.90
Total Assets	27,159,323.64	0.00	11,633,860.00
Liabilities	3,000,000.00	0.00	0.00
Equity			
Common Shares	22,548,340.00	0.00	11,165,120.00
Retained Earnings	1,610,983,64	0.00	468,748.70
Total	27,159,323.64	0.00	11,633,860.00

Press return to continue

- Liabilities

TECHTIME's loan of $2,000,000 has been added to PROTIME's $1,000,000 indebtedness to total $3,000,000.

- Common Shares

Common shares are simply those of PROTIME before the takeover.

- Retained Earnings

The difference between PROTIME's retained earnings before and after the takeover is the profit or loss of the takeover itself. The retained earnings are increased or decreased by the difference in cash, increased by the **net** capital equipment, and decreased by the increased indebtedness. (The Net Capital Equipment of TECHTIME was $1,439,640.)

	Retained Earnings Y3 PROTIME	$ 2,232,396
+	difference in cash for PROTIME	(61,062)
+	Net addition of Capital equipment	1,439,640
–	additional indebtedness	– 2,000,000
	PROTIME's Retained Earnings post Takeover (minor discrepancy due to rounding in the program)	$ 1,610,974

Liquidity And Performance Measure For PROTIME

After takeover these indicators are calculated just as shown above, with the exceptions that:

1. The post takeover balance sheet entries would be employed in the calculations.
2. The Y3 net income used in the performance measures is the pre takeover net income of PROTIME plus the gain or minus the loss in retained earnings.

Comments On The Takeover

It is arguable whether PROTIME acted wisely in acquiring TECHTIME. On the one hand, the company experienced a paper loss and small cash loss on the transaction. Due to these losses, PROTIME's shares would now have no market value. However, a competitor has also been eliminated. The answer to the question really revolves around whether ELEKTRIX or PROTIME may benefit the most. Given that PROTIME's resources are significantly superior, they may now be able to concentrate fully upon either acquiring ELEKTRIX, or driving them into bankruptcy. ELEKTRIX, on the other hand, may now have an easier job to design a survival strategy with just one competitor who has been somewhat weakened by a risky acquisition.

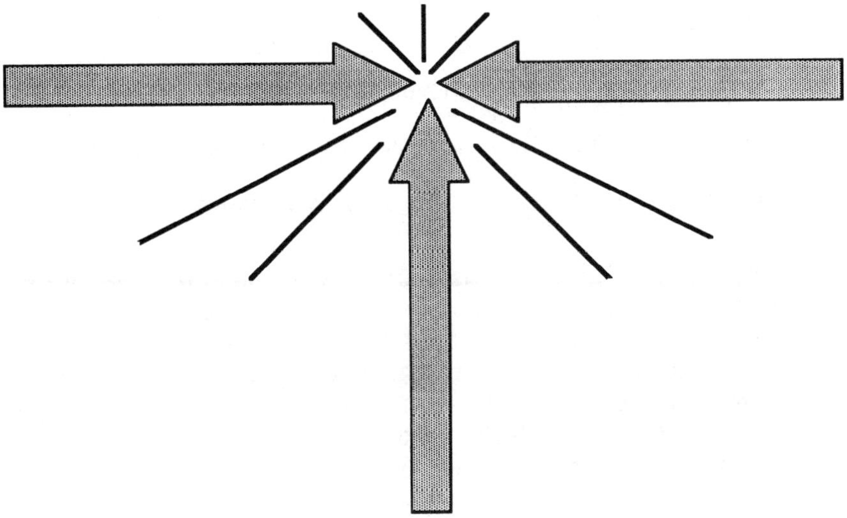

PART IV - STRATEGIC CONTROL

24. A METHOD OF STRATEGIC CONTROL

A Strategic Control System must be able to identify, diagnose and correct deficiencies in the strategic planning, formulation, and implementation processes. These deficiencies are inevitable due to limitations in the accuracy of information employed, as well as to the inherent complexity in analyzing the data, formulating a strategy, and devising an appropriate implementation sequence. The strategic control system is therefore that part of the strategic process upon which the attainment of effective performance finally depends. Even the most competent formulation of strategy is likely to be relatively ineffective in achievement, if there is a lack of fine-tuning afforded by the strategic control system.

Strategic Control is comprised of three stages: Assessment, or evaluation of current performance; Diagnosis, or the identification of the cause and effect relationship between the strategy as it was implemented and the results obtained; and Correction, or the modification of strategy to remedy deficiencies in performance. Assessment will naturally take place first and it should be carried out on a pro-active basis. An investigation of performance should proceed regardless of whether planned-for results are achieved. An easy attainment of objectives that have been set too low is also an indication of faulty planning.

Assessment

The Assessment of Performance can consist of the answers to three questions in all areas for which objectives were set as follows:

A. Were the objectives overachieved, achieved, or underachieved?

B. Did the allocation of resources to meet those objectives take place as planned?

C. Were the planned policies and procedures actually adhered to?

Since the assessment begins with a comparison between planned and actual performance, it is necessary to have formulated a well thought out set of goals during the planning process. If an objective (quantitative) format was used for these goals, it is easy to assess the extent of their achievement. Next is a check as to whether the resources that were intended to be used when the objectives were set, were actually deployed. For example, was the planned expenditure on capital equipment made? Did the firm decide at the last minute to use cheaper raw materials? When any element of a plan is altered, results orginally contemplated may not be attainable. Finally, step C examines whether all planned work procedures were faithfully implemented. In a real company, this stage of the assessment can extend to examination of how all exmployees carried out their jobs. In CONFRONTATION there is, of course, no actual implementation of the required day-to-day work procedures required to maintain a company in operation. However, complex planning procedures requiring the effective collaboration of all simulation participants may or may not have been rigorously followed. If not, that may very well have been a contributing factor of great significance to the nonachievement of objectives.

Diagnosis

The purpose of the above questions is to provide useful data for the diagnostic stage. Each firm in the simulation must set specific targets in all areas of operations, allocate resources in an appropriate manner, and prescribe certain procedures to work out policies in each functional area. Unless the strategic process is rigorously completed in this manner, diagnosis of strategic errors and correction to improve performance cannot be adequately accomplished. For example, suppose that during a given year a firm has made a larger profit than anticipated. Then suppose that the reason this occurred was that the high market was experienced. If the firm had purchased a market survey, found out that the higher market was very likely, and accordingly planned a more aggressive strategy, then its profit objective should have been higher, and its actual performance would have been much improved. In the case when such improvement exceeds the cost of the survey, the correct policy would have been to purchase the survey. Therefore, the firm's analytical procedures are faulty in respect of the market survey. However, if management is not skeptical, even of success, and if they do not examine resource allocations and work procedures in addition to whether objectives are met, this strategic mistake would never come to light.

Table 2 below gives general indications as to what type of diagnoses may result from the range of answers to the three questions concerning objectives, resources and procedures. A specific diagnosis (as in the above example) will be easier to formulate if the likely generic indications are used as first approximations to be verified, and then fleshed out or discarded. Following are the generic interpretations referred to in Table 2 below.

A. Inaccurate assessment of the environmental determinants of strategy. In CONFRONTATION, these include competitors' resources, competitors' behaviour, and market data.

B. Over- or underestimation of the firm's resources, and their capacity to support the chosen strategy. This includes the potential resource of additional working capital that exists due to the firm's borrowing power or its ability to issue shares.

C. Strategic planning procedures that do not properly evaluate environmental factors and internal resources with respect to what are the appropriate objectives.

D. A formulation of strategic decisions (including resource allocations) that do not enable the firm to meet its objectives. In other words, it is a poorly formulated set of strategic decisions.

Correction

Corrective action must first apply to the way in which management (students) carries out strategic planning and then to the strategic decisions themselves. Obviously, the purpose of altering the method of strategic planning is to improve the resultant decisions. In the simulation, when the same information is readily available to each firm, the different methods of strategic planning and the resulting differences in effectiveness will be the way in which one firm will emerge as the most successful. If the strategic control system can improve the planning process, that will be its most important function. Analogous to the four generic diagnoses given above, are the following generic corrections. These should be employed to generally indicate the ways in which the strategic planning process might be improved. The specific corrections required will come to light through a determination by management of whether the generic corrections apply, and how to make a detailed alteration in the process of formulating strategy. The better decisions that will be made may well result in improved performance.

X. Conduct a more thorough examination of the external determinants of strategy. Check to ensure that competitors' behaviour is as accurately forecasted as possible; that competitors' resources (and potential resources) are fully considered; and assess whether purchasing a market survey appears to be profitable.

Y. Reassess the capability of your firm's resources to accomplish the strategic mission. Ensure that resources are in the appropriate form and are correctly allocated. Note that resource transformations such as cash to inventory, borrowing power to cash, or cash to capital equipment may be necessary to achieve the appropriate mix.

Z. Review strategic planning methods with the aim of attaining a more accurate and a more rigorous analysis. Commonly, the following procedures may be neglected or dealt with incompletely.

- Consideration of the entire likely range of competitors' future behaviour, instead of narrowly considering only what each has done before.

- Searching for and identifying worst and best case scenarios among chosen strategies in order to test for unacceptably poor and extraordinarily good potential outcomes. Even though a selective analysis of this nature can be time consuming, it is necessary in order that unacceptable risks can be avoided and very attractive outcomes made more probable. Too often, management only considers a narrow range of alternatives centered about what was done previously – whether it was successful or not. Then, only average results may be expected; despite that relatively more favourable outcomes may perhaps be attainable, given a broader analysis. Broadening the scope of situations considered and outcomes that may be experienced is often a valuable corrective action. Commonly encountered examples of incomplete analysis include lack of consideration for altering the product's price range or obtaining a market survey when the previous strategy can be profitably altered.

- If the strategic analysis is not sufficiently rigorous for the above or any other reasons, then perhaps the work is not well organized among the management group. The amount and depth of analysis required by the simulation puts great emphasis upon the proper coordination of management resources.

Table 2
Possible Generic Indications for A Strategic Control System

Strategic Objectives Met?	Planned Resources Allocated?	Proper Planning Procedures Followed?	Diagnostic Indication	Corrective Indication
Yes	Yes	Yes	Perhaps A, B?	Perhaps Z?
Yes	No	Yes	Likely B, D	Likely Y, Z
Yes	Yes	No	Likely C, Z	Likely X, Z
Yes	No	No	Likely B, C	Likely Y, Z
No	Yes	Yes	Likely A, B, C,	Likely X,Y, Z
No	No	Yes	Likely D	Likely Y, Z
No	Yes	No	Likely C, D	Likely Z
No	No	No	Failure of Strategic Planning. Rebuild entire process.	Failure of Strategic Planning. Rebuild entire process.

Each suggested Diagnostic or Corrective indication may be considered as just a starting point for the investigation of what might have gone wrong and how it may be remedied. The indicators should suggest likely lines of inquiry that may yield results when working with specific instances of performance or non performance. The most important point is to realize that strategic planning is a very difficult task to perfect. Continual striving to correct deficiencies and to improve previous planning methods is the way to ultimately achieve excellence in this crucial business activity.

25. AN ILLUSTRATIVE EXAMPLE OF STRATEGIC CONTROL

Referring back to the Cash Budget Work Sheet of PROTIME on p. 42, the firm predicted sales revenue of $9,509,000, whereas in reality only $6,570,000 in sales was actually achieved. Suppose now that the resources the company allocated on p. 40 were in accordance with their original plan. Secondly, suppose that the firm had followed all of its usual planning procedures, which included the calculation of a number of projected economic scenarios. Not even the worst case of these apparently predicted that sales would be as low as that received, and that profits would be as poor as the loss of over $1,000,000, which was actually incurred.

It could perhaps be argued that since the year ended with a takeover of TECHTIME, and that this outcome was a likely goal as well, that there was a fair achievement of objectives. Note that PROTIME was close to winning the simulation, since it was nearly possible to takeover ELEKTRIX as well (see p. 56). If PROTIME had earned a substantial profit and/or inflicted a much more substantial loss upon Elektrix, that might have been the result. Thus, the objective could have been to win the simulation by taking over both competitors.

Referring to Table 2, the fifth line of generic indications seems appropriate. The most likely generic diagnosis, then, would be:

A. An inaccurate environmental assessment; or

B. An inaccurate resource assessment; or

C. Improper strategic planning procedures;

or a combination of the above.

With respect to A, the firm did not purchase a market survey and therefore planned for a normal size market. This was not a problem since the market size was normal (although it could have been, since the effect of a high market is more pronounced in the high quality segment). Generally, the position and policies of each competitive firm was really quite similar in each of the previous years. Presumably, PROTIME was adequately aware of the environmental situation. Diagnosis A may be ruled out as a likely conclusion.

For B, the resource assessment, there seems to be grounds for constructive criticism of the previous assessment of resource competence. Although PROTIME knew it would begin the year with over $20,000,000 of additional working capital from an equity issue, there is little evidence that the Maxigain type strategy it tried to employ really contemplated the resource strength it could have brought to bear.

Finally, in terms of C, the strategic planning procedures, obviously something has gone wrong. PROTIME was alone in the high quality market segment; it was heavily endowed with working capital; its competitors did nothing very drastic; and yet it suffered a relatively heavy loss. The method of projecting and calculating economic scenarios should be examined very carefully. Either the not unusual competitive situation that occurred was overlooked, or its results were incorrectly calculated.

Following the identification of probable faults under B and C in the diagnostic stage, appropriate corrective measures should include:

Y. Reassessment of resource competence; and

Z. Revision of strategic planning procedures.

Measure Z seems especially important for PROTIME as they may have failed to win the simulation in year 3 by taking over both competitors, simply through failing to correctly examine all strategic situations. They should specifically revise their methods of selecting economic scenarios for evaluation, with the intention of including a broader range of possible situations. Secondly, PROTIME should check that their calculations of the performance results for each scenario they examine is carried out accurately, and correct the methods of calculation accordingly.

Note that this example of exercising strategic control is abbreviated, and meant only to illustrate suggested methods and the means by which generic indications can be translated into specific conclusions and measures. In a full treatment, PROTIME might find several other areas requiring attention in the diagnostic stage. Corrections to be applied should specify in detail how existing methods are to be altered.

NOTES

NOTES

NOTES

NOTES

NOTES

NOTES

Strategic Decision Form For Year ________

Market Assumption High / Normal / No Survey

Company Name ____________________

Year ____________________

President ____________________

Analysts(s) ____________________

____

____

Marketing Manager ____________________

Production Manager ____________________

Engineering Manager ____________________

Design Manager ____________________

FINANCIAL AND PROMOTIONAL DECISIONS

Issue of Shares # ____________

Increase Loan by $ / or Decrease Loan by $ ____________

Financial Investment / A or B $ ____________ /A or B

Capital Equipment Investment $ ____________

Advertising Expenditure $ ____________

BUDGETARY ALLOCATIONS

Marketing Department $ ____________

Production Department $ ____________

Engineering Department $ ____________

Design Department $ ____________

General and Administration $ 250,000

SALES AND PRODUCTION DECISIONS

Product Price $ ____________

Raw Material Cost $ ____________

Minimum Yearly Sales # ____________

Production Quantity # ____________

Strategic Decision Form   For Year ________

Market Assumption   High / Normal / No Survey

Company Name ______________________________

Year ______________________________

President ______________________________

Analysts(s) ______________________________

____

____

Marketing Manager ______________________________

Production Manager ______________________________

Engineering Manager ______________________________

Design Manager ______________________________

FINANCIAL AND PROMOTIONAL DECISIONS

Issue of Shares	# ________
Increase Loan by $ / or Decrease Loan by	$ ________
Financial Investment / A or B	$ ________ /A or B
Capital Equipment Investment	$ ________
Advertising Expenditure	$ ________

BUDGETARY ALLOCATIONS

Marketing Department	$ ________
Production Department	$ ________
Engineering Department	$ ________
Design Department	$ ________
General and Administration	$ 250,000

SALES AND PRODUCTION DECISIONS

Product Price	$ ________
Raw Material Cost	$ ________
Minimum Yearly Sales	# ________
Production Quantity	# ________

Strategic Decision Form For Year ________

Market Assumption High / Normal / No Survey

Company Name	______________________
Year	______________________
President	______________________
Analysts(s)	______________________
	______________________
	______________________
Marketing Manager	______________________
Production Manager	______________________
Engineering Manager	______________________
Design Manager	______________________

FINANCIAL AND PROMOTIONAL DECISIONS

Issue of Shares	# ____________
Increase Loan by $ / or Decrease Loan by	$ ____________
Financial Investment / A or B	$ ____________ /A or B
Capital Equipment Investment	$ ____________
Advertising Expenditure	$ ____________

BUDGETARY ALLOCATIONS

Marketing Department	$ ____________
Production Department	$ ____________
Engineering Department	$ ____________
Design Department	$ ____________
General and Administration	$ 250,000

SALES AND PRODUCTION DECISIONS

Product Price	$ ____________
Raw Material Cost	$ ____________
Minimum Yearly Sales	# ____________
Production Quantity	# ____________

Strategic Decision Form   For Year ________

Market Assumption   High / Normal / No Survey

Company Name	______________________
Year	______________________
President	______________________
Analysts(s)	______________________
	______________________
	______________________
Marketing Manager	______________________
Production Manager	______________________
Engineering Manager	______________________
Design Manager	______________________

FINANCIAL AND PROMOTIONAL DECISIONS

Issue of Shares	# ____________
Increase Loan by $ / or Decrease Loan by	$ ____________
Financial Investment / A or B	$ ____________ /A or B
Capital Equipment Investment	$ ____________
Advertising Expenditure	$ ____________

BUDGETARY ALLOCATIONS

Marketing Department	$ ____________
Production Department	$ ____________
Engineering Department	$ ____________
Design Department	$ ____________
General and Administration	$ 250,000

SALES AND PRODUCTION DECISIONS

Product Price	$ ____________
Raw Material Cost	$ ____________
Minimum Yearly Sales	# ____________
Production Quantity	# ____________

Strategic Decision Form   For Year ________

Market Assumption   High / Normal / No Survey

Company Name ______________________

Year ______________________

President ______________________

Analysts(s) ______________________

____

____

Marketing Manager ______________________

Production Manager ______________________

Engineering Manager ______________________

Design Manager ______________________

FINANCIAL AND PROMOTIONAL DECISIONS

Issue of Shares	# ________
Increase Loan by $ / or Decrease Loan by	$ ________
Financial Investment / A or B	$ ________ /A or B
Capital Equipment Investment	$ ________
Advertising Expenditure	$ ________

BUDGETARY ALLOCATIONS

Marketing Department	$ ________
Production Department	$ ________
Engineering Department	$ ________
Design Department	$ ________
General and Administration	$ 250,000

SALES AND PRODUCTION DECISIONS

Product Price	$ ________
Raw Material Cost	$ ________
Minimum Yearly Sales	# ________
Production Quantity	# ________

Strategic Decision Form For Year ________

Market Assumption High / Normal / No Survey

Company Name	________
Year	________
President	________
Analysts(s)	________
	________
	________
Marketing Manager	________
Production Manager	________
Engineering Manager	________
Design Manager	________

FINANCIAL AND PROMOTIONAL DECISIONS

Issue of Shares	# ________
Increase Loan by $ / or Decrease Loan by	$ ________
Financial Investment / A or B	$ ________ /A or B
Capital Equipment Investment	$ ________
Advertising Expenditure	$ ________

BUDGETARY ALLOCATIONS

Marketing Department	$ ________
Production Department	$ ________
Engineering Department	$ ________
Design Department	$ ________
General and Administration	$ 250,000

SALES AND PRODUCTION DECISIONS

Product Price	$ ________
Raw Material Cost	$ ________
Minimum Yearly Sales	# ________
Production Quantity	# ________

Strategic Decision Form   For Year ________

Market Assumption   High / Normal / No Survey

Company Name ______________________________

Year ______________________________

President ______________________________

Analysts(s) ______________________________

____

____

Marketing Manager ______________________________

Production Manager ______________________________

Engineering Manager ______________________________

Design Manager ______________________________

FINANCIAL AND PROMOTIONAL DECISIONS

Issue of Shares	# ________
Increase Loan by $ / or Decrease Loan by	$ ________
Financial Investment / A or B	$ ________ /A or B
Capital Equipment Investment	$ ________
Advertising Expenditure	$ ________

BUDGETARY ALLOCATIONS

Marketing Department	$ ________
Production Department	$ ________
Engineering Department	$ ________
Design Department	$ ________
General and Administration	$ 250,000

SALES AND PRODUCTION DECISIONS

Product Price	$ ________
Raw Material Cost	$ ________
Minimum Yearly Sales	# ________
Production Quantity	# ________

Strategic Decision Form For Year ________

Market Assumption High / Normal / No Survey

Company Name ______________________

Year ______________________

President ______________________

Analysts(s) ______________________

____

____

Marketing Manager ______________________

Production Manager ______________________

Engineering Manager ______________________

Design Manager ______________________

FINANCIAL AND PROMOTIONAL DECISIONS

Issue of Shares # ____________

Increase Loan by $ / or Decrease Loan by $ ____________

Financial Investment / A or B $ ____________ /A or B

Capital Equipment Investment $ ____________

Advertising Expenditure $ ____________

BUDGETARY ALLOCATIONS

Marketing Department $ ____________

Production Department $ ____________

Engineering Department $ ____________

Design Department $ ____________

General and Administration $ 250,000

SALES AND PRODUCTION DECISIONS

Product Price $ ____________

Raw Material Cost $ ____________

Minimum Yearly Sales # ____________

Production Quantity # ____________

Cash Budget Worksheet   For Year ________

	$	$	
Sources of Cash at Beginning of Year			
Starting Cash	________		
Proceeds of New Equity Issue	________		
Loan Capital	________		
Total Cash Sources at Beginning of Year		________	(1)
Cash Committed at Beginning of Year			
Repayment of Loan	________		
Purchase of Capital Equipment	________		
Advertising Expenditure	________		
Purchase of Market Survey	________		
Departmental Budgetary Allocations	________		
General and Administration Allocation	________		
External Financial Investment	________		
Total Cash Committed at Beginning of Year		________	(2)
Net Cash at Beginning of Year (1) – (2) [(3) Must be a positive number]		________	(3)
Planned Production x 1/2 Raw Material Cost/Unit [(3) must not be less than (4) if there is a financial investment]		________	(4)
Impact of Sales			
Expected Sales Revenue	________		
less Total Raw Material Expense	________		
Inventory Expenses	________		
Sales Revenue net of Variable Costs		________	(5)
Expected Revenue from Financial Investment plus Principal		________	(6)
Net Cash before Tax and Profit Sharing [(3) + (5) + (6)]		________	(7)
Final Expenditures			
Interest Expense	________		
Income Tax	________		
Estimated Profit sharing	________		
Total End of Year Cash Deductions	________ (8)		
Final Cash Position (7) – (8)		________	

Pro Forma Income Statement

For Year _____

Production Capacity	________
Production in Units	________
Sales in Units	________
Sales Revenue	$ ________
Cost of Goods Sold	$ ________
Gross Margin	$ ________
Indirect Costs	$ ________
Advertising	$ ________
Depreciation	$ ________
Design Overhead	$ ________
Engineering Overhead	$ ________
General and Administration	$ ________
Interest Expense	$ ________
Inventory Expense	$ ________
Inventory Write Down	$ ________
Marketing Overhead	$ ________
Market Survey	$ ________
Production Overhead	$ ________
Total Indirect Costs	$ ________
Profit Sharing	$ ________
Net Operating Profit	$ ________
Investment Income	$ ________
Net Profit (before tax)	$ ________
Income Tax	$ ________
Net Profit (after tax)	$ ________

Pro Forma Balance Sheet

Assets		Liabilities and Equity	
Assets	$	Liabilities	$ ________
Cash	________	Equity	
Inventory	________	Common Shares	________
Capital Equipment	________	Retained Earnings	________
Less Depreciation	________	Total Equity	________
Total Assets	$ ________	Total Liabilities plus Equity	$ ________

Cash Budget Worksheet

For Year ________

	$	$	
Sources of Cash at Beginning of Year			
Starting Cash	________		
Proceeds of New Equity Issue	________		
Loan Capital	________		
Total Cash Sources at Beginning of Year		________	(1)
Cash Committed at Beginning of Year			
Repayment of Loan	________		
Purchase of Capital Equipment	________		
Advertising Expenditure	________		
Purchase of Market Survey	________		
Departmental Budgetary Allocations	________		
General and Administration Allocation	________		
External Financial Investment	________		
Total Cash Committed at Beginning of Year		________	(2)
Net Cash at Beginning of Year (1) – (2) [(3) Must be a positive number]		________	(3)
Planned Production x 1/2 Raw Material Cost/Unit [(3) must not be less than (4) if there is a financial investment]		________	(4)
Impact of Sales			
Expected Sales Revenue	________		
less Total Raw Material Expense	________		
Inventory Expenses	________		
Sales Revenue net of Variable Costs		________	(5)
Expected Revenue from Financial Investment plus Principal		________	(6)
Net Cash before Tax and Profit Sharing [(3) + (5) + (6)]		________	(7)
Final Expenditures			
Interest Expense	________		
Income Tax	________		
Estimated Profit sharing	________		
Total End of Year Cash Deductions	________ (8)		
Final Cash Position (7) – (8)		________	

Pro Forma Income Statement

For Year _____

Production Capacity	____________
Production in Units	____________
Sales in Units	____________
Sales Revenue	$ ____________
Cost of Goods Sold	$ ____________
Gross Margin	$ ____________
Indirect Costs	$ ____________
Advertising	$ ____________
Depreciation	$ ____________
Design Overhead	$ ____________
Engineering Overhead	$ ____________
General and Administration	$ ____________
Interest Expense	$ ____________
Inventory Expense	$ ____________
Inventory Write Down	$ ____________
Marketing Overhead	$ ____________
Market Survey	$ ____________
Production Overhead	$ ____________
Total Indirect Costs	$ ____________
Profit Sharing	$ ____________
Net Operating Profit	$ ____________
Investment Income	$ ____________
Net Profit (before tax)	$ ____________
Income Tax	$ ____________
Net Profit (after tax)	$ ____________

Pro Forma Balance Sheet

Assets		Liabilities and Equity	
Assets	$	Liabilities	$ ____________
Cash	____________	Equity	
Inventory	____________	Common Shares	____________
Capital Equipment	____________	Retained Earnings	____________
Less Depreciation	____________	Total Equity	____________
Total Assets	$ ____________	Total Liabilities plus Equity	$ ____________

Cash Budget Worksheet   For Year _______

	$	$	
Sources of Cash at Beginning of Year			
Starting Cash	________		
Proceeds of New Equity Issue	________		
Loan Capital	________		
Total Cash Sources at Beginning of Year		________	(1)
Cash Committed at Beginning of Year			
Repayment of Loan	________		
Purchase of Capital Equipment	________		
Advertising Expenditure	________		
Purchase of Market Survey	________		
Departmental Budgetary Allocations	________		
General and Administration Allocation	________		
External Financial Investment	________		
Total Cash Committed at Beginning of Year		________	(2)
Net Cash at Beginning of Year (1) – (2) [(3) Must be a positive number]		________	(3)
Planned Production x 1/2 Raw Material Cost/Unit [(3) must not be less than (4) if there is a financial investment]		________	(4)
Impact of Sales			
Expected Sales Revenue	________		
less Total Raw Material Expense	________		
Inventory Expenses	________		
Sales Revenue net of Variable Costs		________	(5)
Expected Revenue from Financial Investment plus Principal		________	(6)
Net Cash before Tax and Profit Sharing [(3) + (5) + (6)]		________	(7)
Final Expenditures			
Interest Expense	________		
Income Tax	________		
Estimated Profit sharing	________		
Total End of Year Cash Deductions	________ (8)		
Final Cash Position (7) – (8)		________	

Pro Forma Income Statement For Year _____

Production Capacity	________
Production in Units	________
Sales in Units	________
Sales Revenue	$ ________
Cost of Goods Sold	$ ________
Gross Margin	$ ________
Indirect Costs	$ ________
Advertising	$ ________
Depreciation	$ ________
Design Overhead	$ ________
Engineering Overhead	$ ________
General and Administration	$ ________
Interest Expense	$ ________
Inventory Expense	$ ________
Inventory Write Down	$ ________
Marketing Overhead	$ ________
Market Survey	$ ________
Production Overhead	$ ________
Total Indirect Costs	$ ________
Profit Sharing	$ ________
Net Operating Profit	$ ________
Investment Income	$ ________
Net Profit (before tax)	$ ________
Income Tax	$ ________
Net Profit (after tax)	$ ________

Pro Forma Balance Sheet

Assets		Liabilities and Equity	
Assets	$	Liabilities	$ ________
Cash	________	Equity	
Inventory	________	Common Shares	________
Capital Equipment	________	Retained Earnings	________
Less Depreciation	________	Total Equity	________
Total Assets	$ ________	Total Liabilities plus Equity	$ ________

Cash Budget Worksheet   For Year ______

	$	$	
Sources of Cash at Beginning of Year			
Starting Cash	______		
Proceeds of New Equity Issue	______		
Loan Capital	______		
Total Cash Sources at Beginning of Year		______	(1)
Cash Committed at Beginning of Year			
Repayment of Loan	______		
Purchase of Capital Equipment	______		
Advertising Expenditure	______		
Purchase of Market Survey	______		
Departmental Budgetary Allocations	______		
General and Administration Allocation	______		
External Financial Investment	______		
Total Cash Committed at Beginning of Year		______	(2)
Net Cash at Beginning of Year (1) – (2) [(3) Must be a positive number]		______	(3)
Planned Production x 1/2 Raw Material Cost/Unit [(3) must not be less than (4) if there is a financial investment]		______	(4)
Impact of Sales			
Expected Sales Revenue	______		
less Total Raw Material Expense	______		
Inventory Expenses	______		
Sales Revenue net of Variable Costs		______	(5)
Expected Revenue from Financial Investment plus Principal		______	(6)
Net Cash before Tax and Profit Sharing [(3) + (5) + (6)]		______	(7)
Final Expenditures			
Interest Expense	______		
Income Tax	______		
Estimated Profit sharing	______		
Total End of Year Cash Deductions	______ (8)		
Final Cash Position (7) – (8)		______	

Pro Forma Income Statement

For Year _____

Production Capacity	________
Production in Units	________
Sales in Units	________
Sales Revenue	$ ________
Cost of Goods Sold	$ ________
Gross Margin	$ ________
Indirect Costs	$ ________
Advertising	$ ________
Depreciation	$ ________
Design Overhead	$ ________
Engineering Overhead	$ ________
General and Administration	$ ________
Interest Expense	$ ________
Inventory Expense	$ ________
Inventory Write Down	$ ________
Marketing Overhead	$ ________
Market Survey	$ ________
Production Overhead	$ ________
Total Indirect Costs	$ ________
Profit Sharing	$ ________
Net Operating Profit	$ ________
Investment Income	$ ________
Net Profit (before tax)	$ ________
Income Tax	$ ________
Net Profit (after tax)	$ ________

Pro Forma Balance Sheet

Assets

Assets	$
Cash	________
Inventory	________
Capital Equipment	________
Less Depreciation	________
Total Assets	$ ________

Liabilities and Equity

Liabilities	$ ________
Equity	
Common Shares	________
Retained Earnings	________
Total Equity	________
Total Liabilities plus Equity	$ ________

Cash Budget Worksheet For Year ______

	$	$	
Sources of Cash at Beginning of Year			
Starting Cash	______		
Proceeds of New Equity Issue	______		
Loan Capital	______		
Total Cash Sources at Beginning of Year		______	(1)
Cash Committed at Beginning of Year			
Repayment of Loan	______		
Purchase of Capital Equipment	______		
Advertising Expenditure	______		
Purchase of Market Survey	______		
Departmental Budgetary Allocations	______		
General and Administration Allocation	______		
External Financial Investment	______		
Total Cash Committed at Beginning of Year		______	(2)
Net Cash at Beginning of Year (1) – (2) [(3) Must be a positive number]		______	(3)
Planned Production x 1/2 Raw Material Cost/Unit [(3) must not be less than (4) if there is a financial investment]		______	(4)
Impact of Sales			
Expected Sales Revenue	______		
less Total Raw Material Expense	______		
Inventory Expenses	______		
Sales Revenue net of Variable Costs		______	(5)
Expected Revenue from Financial Investment plus Principal		______	(6)
Net Cash before Tax and Profit Sharing [(3) + (5) + (6)]		______	(7)
Final Expenditures			
Interest Expense	______		
Income Tax	______		
Estimated Profit sharing	______		
Total End of Year Cash Deductions	______ (8)		
Final Cash Position (7) – (8)		______	

Pro Forma Income Statement

For Year _____

Production Capacity	________
Production in Units	________
Sales in Units	________
Sales Revenue	$ ________
Cost of Goods Sold	$ ________
Gross Margin	$ ________
Indirect Costs	$ ________
Advertising	$ ________
Depreciation	$ ________
Design Overhead	$ ________
Engineering Overhead	$ ________
General and Administration	$ ________
Interest Expense	$ ________
Inventory Expense	$ ________
Inventory Write Down	$ ________
Marketing Overhead	$ ________
Market Survey	$ ________
Production Overhead	$ ________
Total Indirect Costs	$ ________
Profit Sharing	$ ________
Net Operating Profit	$ ________
Investment Income	$ ________
Net Profit (before tax)	$ ________
Income Tax	$ ________
Net Profit (after tax)	$ ________

Pro Forma Balance Sheet

Assets		Liabilities and Equity	
Assets	$	Liabilities	$ ________
Cash	________	Equity	
Inventory	________	Common Shares	________
Capital Equipment	________	Retained Earnings	________
Less Depreciation	________	Total Equity	________
Total Assets	$ ________	Total Liabilities plus Equity	$ ________

Cash Budget Worksheet   For Year ________

	$	$	
Sources of Cash at Beginning of Year			
Starting Cash	________		
Proceeds of New Equity Issue	________		
Loan Capital	________		
Total Cash Sources at Beginning of Year		________	(1)
Cash Committed at Beginning of Year			
Repayment of Loan	________		
Purchase of Capital Equipment	________		
Advertising Expenditure	________		
Purchase of Market Survey	________		
Departmental Budgetary Allocations	________		
General and Administration Allocation	________		
External Financial Investment	________		
Total Cash Committed at Beginning of Year		________	(2)
Net Cash at Beginning of Year (1) – (2) [(3) Must be a positive number]		________	(3)
Planned Production x 1/2 Raw Material Cost/Unit [(3) must not be less than (4) if there is a financial investment]		________	(4)
Impact of Sales			
Expected Sales Revenue	________		
less Total Raw Material Expense	________		
Inventory Expenses	________		
Sales Revenue net of Variable Costs		________	(5)
Expected Revenue from Financial Investment plus Principal		________	(6)
Net Cash before Tax and Profit Sharing [(3) + (5) + (6)]		________	(7)
Final Expenditures			
Interest Expense	________		
Income Tax	________		
Estimated Profit sharing	________		
Total End of Year Cash Deductions	________ (8)		
Final Cash Position (7) – (8)		________	

Pro Forma Income Statement

For Year ______

Production Capacity	______
Production in Units	______
Sales in Units	______
Sales Revenue	$ ______
Cost of Goods Sold	$ ______
Gross Margin	$ ______
Indirect Costs	$ ______
Advertising	$ ______
Depreciation	$ ______
Design Overhead	$ ______
Engineering Overhead	$ ______
General and Administration	$ ______
Interest Expense	$ ______
Inventory Expense	$ ______
Inventory Write Down	$ ______
Marketing Overhead	$ ______
Market Survey	$ ______
Production Overhead	$ ______
Total Indirect Costs	$ ______
Profit Sharing	$ ______
Net Operating Profit	$ ______
Investment Income	$ ______
Net Profit (before tax)	$ ______
Income Tax	$ ______
Net Profit (after tax)	$ ______

Pro Forma Balance Sheet

Assets		Liabilities and Equity	
Assets	$	Liabilities	$ ______
Cash	______	Equity	
Inventory	______	Common Shares	______
Capital Equipment	______	Retained Earnings	______
Less Depreciation	______	Total Equity	______
Total Assets	$ ______	Total Liabilities plus Equity	$ ______

Cash Budget Worksheet

For Year ________

	$	$	
Sources of Cash at Beginning of Year			
Starting Cash	________		
Proceeds of New Equity Issue	________		
Loan Capital	________		
Total Cash Sources at Beginning of Year		________	(1)
Cash Committed at Beginning of Year			
Repayment of Loan	________		
Purchase of Capital Equipment	________		
Advertising Expenditure	________		
Purchase of Market Survey	________		
Departmental Budgetary Allocations	________		
General and Administration Allocation	________		
External Financial Investment	________		
Total Cash Committed at Beginning of Year		________	(2)
Net Cash at Beginning of Year (1) – (2) [(3) Must be a positive number]		________	(3)
Planned Production x 1/2 Raw Material Cost/Unit [(3) must not be less than (4) if there is a financial investment]		________	(4)
Impact of Sales			
Expected Sales Revenue	________		
less Total Raw Material Expense	________		
Inventory Expenses	________		
Sales Revenue net of Variable Costs		________	(5)
Expected Revenue from Financial Investment plus Principal		________	(6)
Net Cash before Tax and Profit Sharing [(3) + (5) + (6)]		________	(7)
Final Expenditures			
Interest Expense	________		
Income Tax	________		
Estimated Profit sharing	________		
Total End of Year Cash Deductions	________ (8)		
Final Cash Position (7) – (8)		________	

Pro Forma Income Statement

For Year _____

Production Capacity	________
Production in Units	________
Sales in Units	________
Sales Revenue	$ ________
Cost of Goods Sold	$ ________
Gross Margin	$ ________
Indirect Costs	$ ________
Advertising	$ ________
Depreciation	$ ________
Design Overhead	$ ________
Engineering Overhead	$ ________
General and Administration	$ ________
Interest Expense	$ ________
Inventory Expense	$ ________
Inventory Write Down	$ ________
Marketing Overhead	$ ________
Market Survey	$ ________
Production Overhead	$ ________
Total Indirect Costs	$ ________
Profit Sharing	$ ________
Net Operating Profit	$ ________
Investment Income	$ ________
Net Profit (before tax)	$ ________
Income Tax	$ ________
Net Profit (after tax)	$ ________

Pro Forma Balance Sheet

Assets		Liabilities and Equity	
Assets	$	Liabilities	$ ________
Cash	________	Equity	
Inventory	________	Common Shares	________
Capital Equipment	________	Retained Earnings	________
Less Depreciation	________	Total Equity	________
Total Assets	$ ________	Total Liabilities plus Equity	$ ________

Cash Budget Worksheet For Year ________

	$		$	
Sources of Cash at Beginning of Year				
Starting Cash	________			
Proceeds of New Equity Issue	________			
Loan Capital	________			
Total Cash Sources at Beginning of Year			________	(1)
Cash Committed at Beginning of Year				
Repayment of Loan	________			
Purchase of Capital Equipment	________			
Advertising Expenditure	________			
Purchase of Market Survey	________			
Departmental Budgetary Allocations	________			
General and Administration Allocation	________			
External Financial Investment	________			
Total Cash Committed at Beginning of Year			________	(2)
Net Cash at Beginning of Year (1) – (2) [(3) Must be a positive number]			________	(3)
Planned Production x 1/2 Raw Material Cost/Unit [(3) must not be less than (4) if there is a financial investment]			________	(4)
Impact of Sales				
Expected Sales Revenue	________			
less Total Raw Material Expense	________			
Inventory Expenses	________			
Sales Revenue net of Variable Costs			________	(5)
Expected Revenue from Financial Investment plus Principal			________	(6)
Net Cash before Tax and Profit Sharing [(3) + (5) + (6)]			________	(7)
Final Expenditures				
Interest Expense	________			
Income Tax	________			
Estimated Profit sharing	________			
Total End of Year Cash Deductions	________	(8)		
Final Cash Position (7) – (8)			________	

Pro Forma Income Statement

For Year _____

Production Capacity	
Production in Units	
Sales in Units	
Sales Revenue	$
Cost of Goods Sold	$
Gross Margin	$
Indirect Costs	$
Advertising	$
Depreciation	$
Design Overhead	$
Engineering Overhead	$
General and Administration	$
Interest Expense	$
Inventory Expense	$
Inventory Write Down	$
Marketing Overhead	$
Market Survey	$
Production Overhead	$
Total Indirect Costs	$
Profit Sharing	$
Net Operating Profit	$
Investment Income	$
Net Profit (before tax)	$
Income Tax	$
Net Profit (after tax)	$

Pro Forma Balance Sheet

Assets		Liabilities and Equity	
Assets	$	Liabilities	$
Cash		Equity	
Inventory		Common Shares	
Capital Equipment		Retained Earnings	
Less Depreciation		Total Equity	
Total Assets	$	Total Liabilities plus Equity	$

Economic Scenario Worksheet

For Year ________

Assumed Market Size High ________ Normal ________

	Your Firm	Competitor 1	Competitor 2
	________	________	________
Market Segment/Price	______/____	______/____	______/____
Advertising Effectiveness	________	________	________
Cost of Raw Materials	________	________	________
Capital Equipment Purchase	________	________	________
Marketing Allocation/RE Factor	______/____	______/____	______/____
Production Allocation/RE Factor	______/____	______/____	______/____
Engineering Allocation/RE Factor	______/____	______/____	______/____
Design Allocation/RE Factor	______/____	______/____	______/____
Marketing RE	________	________	________
Production RE	________	________	________
Engineering RE	________	________	________
Design RE	________	________	________
TRE	________	________	________
High Quality Segment Sales (if any)	________		
Low Quality Segment Sales	________		
Total Loan Required	________	________	________
Interest Expense	________	________	________
Company Sales	________	________	________
Market Penetration	________	________	________
Operating Expenses	________	________	________
Operating Profit	________	________	________
Net Profit After Tax	________	________	________

Use this worksheet to estimate the performance results, given selected basic decisions listed above.

1. Note that some sales may be from inventory.
2. Check the estimated balance sheet changes for your firm and for your competitors to determine risk of bankruptcy or takeover opportunities.

Economic Scenario Worksheet For Year _______

Assumed Market Size High _______ Normal _______

	Your Firm	Competitor 1	Competitor 2
Market Segment/Price	/	/	/
Advertising Effectiveness			
Cost of Raw Materials			
Capital Equipment Purchase			
Marketing Allocation/RE Factor	/	/	/
Production Allocation/RE Factor	/	/	/
Engineering Allocation/RE Factor	/	/	/
Design Allocation/RE Factor	/	/	/
Marketing RE			
Production RE			
Engineering RE			
Design RE			
TRE			
High Quality Segment Sales (if any)			
Low Quality Segment Sales			
Total Loan Required			
Interest Expense			
Company Sales			
Market Penetration			
Operating Expenses			
Operating Profit			
Net Profit After Tax			

Use this worksheet to estimate the performance results, given selected basic decisions listed above.

1. Note that some sales may be from inventory.
2. Check the estimated balance sheet changes for your firm and for your competitors to determine risk of bankruptcy or takeover opportunities.

Economic Scenario Worksheet

For Year ________

Assumed Market Size High ________ Normal ________

	Your Firm	Competitor 1	Competitor 2
	________	________	________
Market Segment/Price	______/____	______/____	______/____
Advertising Effectiveness	________	________	________
Cost of Raw Materials	________	________	________
Capital Equipment Purchase	________	________	________
Marketing Allocation/RE Factor	______/____	______/____	______/____
Production Allocation/RE Factor	______/____	______/____	______/____
Engineering Allocation/RE Factor	______/____	______/____	______/____
Design Allocation/RE Factor	______/____	______/____	______/____
Marketing RE	________	________	________
Production RE	________	________	________
Engineering RE	________	________	________
Design RE	________	________	________
TRE	________	________	________
High Quality Segment Sales (if any)	________		
Low Quality Segment Sales	________		
Total Loan Required	________	________	________
Interest Expense	________	________	________
Company Sales	________	________	________
Market Penetration	________	________	________
Operating Expenses	________	________	________
Operating Profit	________	________	________
Net Profit After Tax	________	________	________

Use this worksheet to estimate the performance results, given selected basic decisions listed above.

1. Note that some sales may be from inventory.
2. Check the estimated balance sheet changes for your firm and for your competitors to determine risk of bankruptcy or takeover opportunities.

Economic Scenario Worksheet

For Year ________

Assumed Market Size High ________ Normal ________

	Your Firm	Competitor 1	Competitor 2
Market Segment/Price	________/____	________/____	________/____
Advertising Effectiveness	________	________	________
Cost of Raw Materials	________	________	________
Capital Equipment Purchase	________	________	________
Marketing Allocation/RE Factor	________/____	________/____	________/____
Production Allocation/RE Factor	________/____	________/____	________/____
Engineering Allocation/RE Factor	________/____	________/____	________/____
Design Allocation/RE Factor	________/____	________/____	________/____
Marketing RE	________	________	________
Production RE	________	________	________
Engineering RE	________	________	________
Design RE	________	________	________
TRE	________	________	________

High Quality Segment Sales (if any) ________________

Low Quality Segment Sales ________________

	Your Firm	Competitor 1	Competitor 2
Total Loan Required	________	________	________
Interest Expense	________	________	________
Company Sales	________	________	________
Market Penetration	________	________	________
Operating Expenses	________	________	________
Operating Profit	________	________	________
Net Profit After Tax	________	________	________

Use this worksheet to estimate the performance results, given selected basic decisions listed above.

1. Note that some sales may be from inventory.
2. Check the estimated balance sheet changes for your firm and for your competitors to determine risk of bankruptcy or takeover opportunities.

Economic Scenario Worksheet

For Year ________

Assumed Market Size   High ________   Normal ________

	Your Firm	Competitor 1	Competitor 2
	________	________	________
Market Segment/Price	____/____	____/____	____/____
Advertising Effectiveness	________	________	________
Cost of Raw Materials	________	________	________
Capital Equipment Purchase	________	________	________
Marketing Allocation/RE Factor	____/____	____/____	____/____
Production Allocation/RE Factor	____/____	____/____	____/____
Engineering Allocation/RE Factor	____/____	____/____	____/____
Design Allocation/RE Factor	____/____	____/____	____/____
Marketing RE	________	________	________
Production RE	________	________	________
Engineering RE	________	________	________
Design RE	________	________	________
TRE	________	________	________

High Quality Segment Sales (if any) ____________

Low Quality Segment Sales ____________

	Your Firm	Competitor 1	Competitor 2
Total Loan Required	________	________	________
Interest Expense	________	________	________
Company Sales	________	________	________
Market Penetration	________	________	________
Operating Expenses	________	________	________
Operating Profit	________	________	________
Net Profit After Tax	________	________	________

Use this worksheet to estimate the performance results, given selected basic decisions listed above.

1. Note that some sales may be from inventory.
2. Check the estimated balance sheet changes for your firm and for your competitors to determine risk of bankruptcy or takeover opportunities.

Economic Scenario Worksheet   For Year ________

Assumed Market Size   High ________   Normal ________

	Your Firm	Competitor 1	Competitor 2
	________	________	________
Market Segment/Price	____/____	____/____	____/____
Advertising Effectiveness	________	________	________
Cost of Raw Materials	________	________	________
Capital Equipment Purchase	________	________	________
Marketing Allocation/RE Factor	____/____	____/____	____/____
Production Allocation/RE Factor	____/____	____/____	____/____
Engineering Allocation/RE Factor	____/____	____/____	____/____
Design Allocation/RE Factor	____/____	____/____	____/____
Marketing RE	________	________	________
Production RE	________	________	________
Engineering RE	________	________	________
Design RE	________	________	________
TRE	________	________	________

High Quality Segment Sales (if any) ____________

Low Quality Segment Sales ____________

	Your Firm	Competitor 1	Competitor 2
Total Loan Required	________	________	________
Interest Expense	________	________	________
Company Sales	________	________	________
Market Penetration	________	________	________
Operating Expenses	________	________	________
Operating Profit	________	________	________
Net Profit After Tax	________	________	________

Use this worksheet to estimate the performance results, given selected basic decisions listed above.

1. Note that some sales may be from inventory.
2. Check the estimated balance sheet changes for your firm and for your competitors to determine risk of bankruptcy or takeover opportunities.

Economic Scenario Worksheet   For Year ________

Assumed Market Size	High ______	Normal ______	
	Your Firm	Competitor 1	Competitor 2
	______	______	______
Market Segment/Price	______/____	______/____	______/____
Advertising Effectiveness	______	______	______
Cost of Raw Materials	______	______	______
Capital Equipment Purchase	______	______	______
Marketing Allocation/RE Factor	______/____	______/____	______/____
Production Allocation/RE Factor	______/____	______/____	______/____
Engineering Allocation/RE Factor	______/____	______/____	______/____
Design Allocation/RE Factor	______/____	______/____	______/____
Marketing RE	______	______	______
Production RE	______	______	______
Engineering RE	______	______	______
Design RE	______	______	______
TRE	______	______	______
High Quality Segment Sales (if any)	______		
Low Quality Segment Sales	______		
Total Loan Required	______	______	______
Interest Expense	______	______	______
Company Sales	______	______	______
Market Penetration	______	______	______
Operating Expenses	______	______	______
Operating Profit	______	______	______
Net Profit After Tax	______	______	______

Use this worksheet to estimate the performance results, given selected basic decisions listed above.

1. Note that some sales may be from inventory.
2. Check the estimated balance sheet changes for your firm and for your competitors to determine risk of bankruptcy or takeover opportunities.

Economic Scenario Worksheet   For Year ______

Assumed Market Size   High ______   Normal ______

	Your Firm	Competitor 1	Competitor 2
Market Segment/Price	/	/	/
Advertising Effectiveness			
Cost of Raw Materials			
Capital Equipment Purchase			
Marketing Allocation/RE Factor	/	/	/
Production Allocation/RE Factor	/	/	/
Engineering Allocation/RE Factor	/	/	/
Design Allocation/RE Factor	/	/	/
Marketing RE			
Production RE			
Engineering RE			
Design RE			
TRE			

High Quality Segment Sales (if any) ______________

Low Quality Segment Sales ______________

	Your Firm	Competitor 1	Competitor 2
Total Loan Required			
Interest Expense			
Company Sales			
Market Penetration			
Operating Expenses			
Operating Profit			
Net Profit After Tax			

Use this worksheet to estimate the performance results, given selected basic decisions listed above.

1. Note that some sales may be from inventory.
2. Check the estimated balance sheet changes for your firm and for your competitors to determine risk of bankruptcy or takeover opportunities.